HOW TO
MAKE
YOURSELF
MISERABLE
FOR THE REST
OF THE CENTURY

HOW TO MAKE YOURSELF MISERABLE FOR THE REST OF THE CENTURY

Another vital training manual by **Dan Greenburg**
(who wrote **HOW TO BE A JEWISH MOTHER**),
with **Marcia Jacobs** (who never wrote anything)

Illustrations conceived and drawn by **Marv Rubin**

The Twenty-first Anniversary Edition

Vintage Books
A Division of Random House
New York

First Vintage Books Edition, June 1987
Revised and Updated

Library of Congress Cataloging-in-Publication Data
Greenburg, Dan.
  How to make yourself miserable for the
rest of the century.
  Rev. ed. of: How to make yourself
miserable. 1966.
  1. Psychology—Anecdotes, facetiae, satire, etc.
I. Jacobs, Marcia. II. Greenburg, Dan. How
to make yourself miserable. III. Title.
PN6231.P785G7   1987   818'.5402   86-46195
ISBN 0-394-75079-9

Manufactured in the United States of America
10 9 8 7 6 5 4 3 2 1

What This Book Will Teach You

Chapter 2: Seven Classic Misery-Making Situations
(Page 18)

Chapter 3: Misery About the Past, the Present and the Future (Page 46)

SECTION II: METHODS TO MISERY WITH OTHERS
(Page 73)

Chapter 4: How to Lose Friends and Alienate People
(Page 73)

Chapter 8: How to Lose Any Remaining Friends
(Page 135)

Introduction to the
New Expanded Edition

Ever since we gave you your first lessons in self-torment and despair way back in 1966, the world has thoughtfully made your misery-making considerably easier. For example:

President Nixon turned out to be a scoundrel and was forced to resign on national television. (It is obvious he was a student of this book.)

Secretary of the Interior Watt thought it might be a neat idea to try and sell off parts of our national parks to oil drillers and strip miners.

President Reagan kidded good-naturedly about nuking the Russians and seemed really miffed when they took him seriously.

Although we've been told until it was coming out our ears how *safe* nuclear power plants were and how we were paranoid to even *think* that something could go wrong with them, a nuclear plant at Three Mile Island and one at Chernobyl nearly had core meltdowns.

Cosmetics firms learned more efficient ways of torturing cute animals to test their products. Animal protection groups became irked, photographed the grisliest cases and routinely mail us snapshots.

As the national deficit tripled and Washington kvetched that the budget was already slashed to the bone and couldn't be cut anymore, we learned our government was paying defense contractors a rather generous $400 apiece for hammers.

A new fad swept the country—putting cyanide into nonprescription drugs and ground glass into baby foods.

We went through a sexual revolution and then had to quickly invent two new venereal diseases that have no cure, one of which is 100 percent fatal.

Some religious folks in the Near East decided that hijacking planes and ships and blowing innocent people to smithereens with *plastique* was a nifty way to get media attention.

Marcia Jacobs got married and divorced and moved to Los Angeles, where she's afraid an earthquake will send her sliding into the Pacific. Dan Greenburg got married, divorced, remarried, became a dad and stayed in New York, where he's afraid to ride the subways.

And in the two decades during which all this was happening, our book continued helping people to feel absolutely wretched—not only in the United States, but through translations, in Sweden, Denmark, Norway, Belgium, Argentina, France and Japan.

Our publishers recently informed us that they were bringing out a new edition and asked us if we'd look over what we'd written back in 1966 and see what we wanted to change or add. This was supposed to have been a *Twentieth* Anniversary edition, but we all procrastinated so long that we had to settle for a *Twenty-first* Anniversary edition, which makes us feel pretty stupid.

There was almost nothing we wanted to change. There was a lot that cried out to be added, on such subjects as herpes, AIDS, the Heimlich maneuver, CPR, word processors, answering machines, the women's movement, Alzheimer's disease, arugula and radicchio and sun-dried tomatoes, airline disasters, aerobic exercise, pregnancy and Lamaze, international terrorism, Uzis, *plastique* and sushi.

The new sections may strike you as being less innocent and more morbid than the old ones, which seems appropriate to us. Let's face it, the world is less innocent and more morbid today than it was back in 1966. In most cases we have labeled the new sections For Advanced Practitioners, so if you are not serious about your masochism, you can just skip right over them.

We hope that you've been well, that the last two decades have afforded you plenty of opportunities for self-torment and heartache, and that it won't be another twenty-one years before we speak again.

—Dan Greenburg, New York City
—Marcia Jacobs, Los Angeles
Spring 1987

HOW TO
MAKE
YOURSELF
MISERABLE
FOR THE REST
OF THE CENTURY

SECTION I:
Methods to Misery Alone

Chapter 1: Basics of Self-Torture

Why You Need to Be Miserable

You, we can safely assume, are guilty.

Guilty of *what* we don't know. Frankly, we don't *want* to know. Chances are it's something pretty tacky.

Perhaps you're toying with the notion of spraying Black Flag on your father's Cheerios, or of running off to Denver with your dearest friend's spouse.

Or maybe it's something more exotic, like secret romantic feelings toward: (1) your locker-mate at the Y, (2) your sister, (3) your Doberman pinscher, (4) your umbrella. (We're willing to give you the benefit of the doubt and assume none of these things has progressed beyond the notion stage.)

3

Well, whatever it is, it's your own business and we don't wish to pry. Our only concern is that you have toyed with a few socially frowned-upon ideas, that you feel guilty about doing so, and that—quite logically—you wish to be punished for your guilt.

Who can you get to punish you—your father? your dearest friend? your locker-mate? Hardly. These people don't even know about your guilt. And besides, they're far too busy punishing *themselves* to be bothered about punishing you. Clearly, if any punishing is to get done, you are going to have to do it yourself.

Well, then how to go about it? How to make yourself as miserable as you truly deserve to be?

You probably already have a few misery-making methods of your own—like bombarding yourself with morbid fears about that persistent pain in your stomach, or berating yourself about what you should have said to that rude salesperson in Heavy Appliances.

Whatever you're now doing to yourself, we can help you do it better.

In this book we shall outline two paths to misery which are at once deadly effective and easy to follow. The first, a solitary pursuit, is *The Creation of Anxieties*. The second, which requires the use of other people as unwitting accomplices, is *Making People Reject You*.

These two techniques, combined in an intensive but sensible program of suffering and self-torture, will be all you need to attain the elusive and much sought-after goal of Total Personal Misery.

And now, on to the first of our two methods to misery.

How to Create a First-Class Anxiety

Do you know how to worry?

Of course you do.

Or do you?

Let us rephrase the question. Do you know how to worry *creatively*? Can you take the simple worries and commonplace fears of everyday life and transform them into true misery-making anxieties?

If not, you can be taught. And the first step is learning how to select a 3-Dimensional Worry.

How to Select a 3-Dimensional Worry

Some worries are just not good anxiety material. For instance, there's little point in fearing a visit to the dentist and the discovery of cavities if you: (a) watch between-meal treats and brush often with an effective decay-preventive dentifrice in a conscientiously applied program of oral hygiene and regular professional care, or (b) have no nerve endings in your mouth, or (c) wear false teeth.

No, in order for a fear to become a 3-Dimensional Worry it must fulfill three important conditions or dimensions:

DIMENSION # 1: *There must be hell to pay if your fear proves to be true.*

DIMENSION #2: *There must be some evidence that your fear* WILL *prove true.*

DIMENSION #3: *There must be a substantial period of time to wait before you can find out if your fear is true.*

Medically based fears *are* among the most promising, but let us select for illustrative purposes here something more ominous than a possible cavity. Let us choose, for example, a fear that you're coming down with an obscure but deadly disease. Could this fear become a 3-Dimensional Worry? It could, provided the disease you've selected can pass certain tests.

DIMENSION #1: Have you chosen a disease which could not only have dangerous complications but which would also require lengthy, expensive, painful and humiliating treatment?

DIMENSION #2: Have you chosen a disease whose early symptoms are so general that you could find them in a common cold and an upset stomach?

DIMENSION #3: Have you chosen a disease whose positive

confirmation would require that you take off from work and spend at least a couple of days undergoing tests in a hospital?

If you can answer "yes" to all of the above questions, then you have a true 3-Dimensional Worry, and you are ready to develop it into a First-Class Anxiety.

Let us assume, however, that you are not quite so fortunate—that your fear has failed to meet one or even two of our prerequisites. Do not be dismayed. You may still be able to supply the missing condition, provided you have mastered the all-important Power of Negative Thinking.

The Power of Negative Thinking

Negative thinking is the ability to picture a little love nest out where the roses cling, and see mortgage payments and rose fever. It is the ability to walk in the shade with your blues on parade, to direct your feet to the *gloomy* side of the street and *not* leave your worries on the doorstep where they can't be of any use to you.

Some people are born with this Power of Negative Thinking. Some—like lawyers—develop it through years of intensive training. Any lawyer can tell you every bad thing that either *has* ever happened or *could* ever happen to someone in your situation, whatever that situation might be.

Since it would not be practical for you to have a lawyer

with you at all times, you must learn to imagine all the disastrous possibilities in all types of situations yourself.

To return to your worry about becoming gravely ill.

Let's say your inability to satisfy all the requirements for a 3-Dimensional Worry stems from the fact that you have had a physical examination within the past three or four months and have been given a clean bill of health. Does this make your situation hopelessly unthreatening?

It emphatically does not. First of all, how can you be sure some serious condition hasn't cropped up *since* your examination?

Second, how can you be sure there wasn't some fact you neglected to tell the doctor, something which you didn't even think was important enough to mention at the time, but which any medical man would have instantly recognized as the tip-off symptom?

Or, even assuming there wasn't a single relevant fact you failed to tell him—how can you be absolutely certain he was competent enough to interpret correctly the information you gave him?

Or, even assuming he was competent, how can you be sure he gave you a *complete* physical examination? How complete *is* a complete physical examination? Couldn't there have been a test—perhaps the very one which would have

FIG. I: BEGINNER'S EXERCISE IN NEGATIVE THINKING

Without referring to the list below, how many potential hazards can you identify in this scene?

Partial List of Hazards: (A) Intense sunlight could fade your clothing, grass could permanently stain it; (B) passing bird could soil on your head; (C) passing airliner could erroneously jettison its septic tank on your car or person; (D) bottles could tip over and spill on clothes; (E) soft drinks could rot your teeth; (F) pollen could inflame your nasal membranes; (G) nearsighted bee, attracted by flower, could accidentally fly into your ear, become trapped and hysterical; (H) weakened tree limb could fall and fracture your skull; (I) sultry weather could cause embarrassment; (J) great distance from nearest restroom could cause extreme anguish; (K) continuous weight of arm could irritate appendix; (L) companion could suddenly realize how boring you are; (M) freelance photographer could snap embarrassing pictures from helicopter; (N) vice-squad officer submerged in stream could be observing you through periscope; (O) thin bear could be lurking behind tree; (P) you could stub your toe on boulder or get tetanus from stepping on rusty nail; (Q) you could break your teeth on smooth white rock you mistook for hardboiled egg; (R) passing Greyhound bus could careen out of control and demolish your car; (S) mischievous passerby could release handbrake, or paint obscenities in permanent enamel; (T) ground tremor could loosen bank; (U) sudden lava flow could engulf you; (V) stray lightning bolt from cloud could strike tree and electrocute you; (W) plant lice from bark could lodge in scalp; (X) flash flood could carry you away; (Y) rabid herring could leap out of stream and attack your toes.

revealed your illness—which he didn't consider worth giving you because the disease was too rare and the test too cumbersome?

Did he, for example, give you a complete set of x-rays, including the so-called "G.I. series"? If not, that's probably the only thing which could have saved you.

Or let's say he *did* take x-rays but found no cause for concern. How can you be sure you didn't move while the machine was on and the plate was being exposed, thereby blurring the image and covering up the subtle, telltale characteristics of your affliction?

Or let's even say you're positive you didn't move while the plate was being exposed. How can you be sure that your x-rays weren't accidentally switched with those of a healthy person by some young intern in the darkroom who was simultaneously developing porno films?

In short, there is no situation that, with the application of a little creative Negative Thinking, cannot be turned into a true 3-Dimensional Worry.*

---

* It's also possible that your doctor discovered you have an incurable fatal disease and has decided not to tell you.

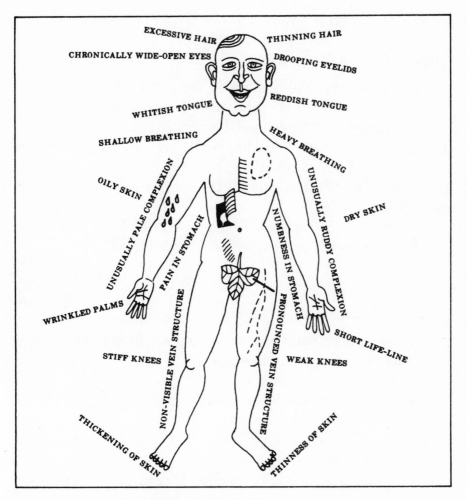

FIG. II: MEDICAL ANXIETY FORMATION GUIDE

How many of these seemingly undangerous symptoms of dread diseases do you have?

How to Mellow Your Worry

Fine worries, like fine wines, are at their best only after they have been properly mellowed. To properly mellow your newly formed 3-Dimensional Worry: dwell on the most unpleasant things that could happen to you if your fear proves to be true; blame yourself for having let the situation progress this far; think about all the ways the situation could have been avoided.

Once your worry has been properly mellowed, you are ready to convert it to a First-Class Anxiety.

Worries into Anxieties

How to take your fear of having an undetected illness that last rewarding step and make it a First-Class Anxiety? There are just three steps:

STEP 1: *Figure out the one way you could find out if your fears are justified.*

STEP 2: *Figure out why the action of finding out is impossible for you to take.*

STEP 3: *Figure out why inaction is equally impossible for you.*

Let's see how these steps apply to your worry.

STEP 1: Obviously, the only way to find out whether your

fears about disease are justified is to submit to that unpleasant two- or three-day hospital examination.

STEP 2: There are a number of reasons why this course of action is impossible for you. We need only mention the threat of finding out something you don't want to know, or the undeniable impossibility of taking off from work for a couple of days to go to the hospital when there's probably nothing wrong with with you at all. And think how embarrassed you'd be after all that fuss to have them find out you're perfectly healthy.*

STEP 3: Of course, if you *are* really ill and you just sit back and don't do anything about it, very soon it will be too *late* to do anything about it—so a course of inaction is equally unthinkable. What should you do? Whatever it is, you must make your decision fast. You don't even know how much time you have left, and the clock is already running out on you.

Now that you have succeeded in making both action and inaction impossible, you will have automatically produced the vital emotion known as Frenzy,† thereby completing the trans-

------

* Should you ever weaken and decide to contact a physician, your symptoms may suddenly disappear. Don't let this alarm you. As soon as the opportunity has passed and it's no longer possible to contact him, your symptoms will reappear.

† An interesting bonus effect of Frenzy is that it can actually *cause* your fears to come true—especially in the lower digestive tract.

formation to Anxiety—because a Mellow 3-Dimensional Worry ($3DW_m$) plus Frenzy (F) are all you need to achieve a First-Class Anxiety (FCA). Or, to put it into terms of the scientist: $3DW_m + F = FCA$.

Exercise in Anxiety

Arrange an important business trip to another town, a trip which could have great bearing on the future of your job.

Make a reservation on a plane leaving at 8:00 A.M. Find out exactly how long it takes to drive from your home to the airport, park your car in the airport parking lot, and board your plane.

Let's say it takes exactly one hour door to door.

The night before your trip, get into your car and keep driving around the block until your gas gauge reads just a notch above the "empty" mark.

The following morning, leave your home at precisely 7:00 A.M.

If traffic is light and you don't encounter any delays, there is a very good chance that you will make your plane. *But if you either run out of gas along the way or stop at a service station, you will surely miss your plane.*

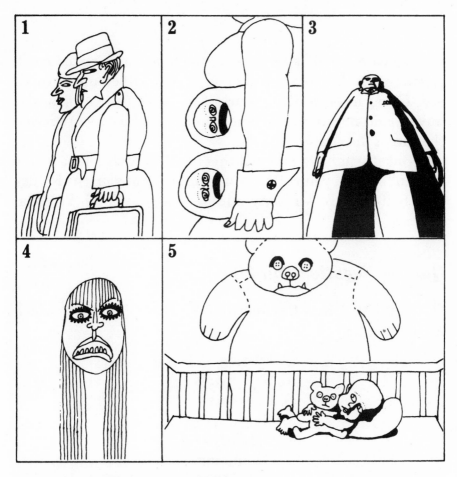

FIG. III: BASIC WORRIES FOR THE VERY YOUNG

(1) Mommy and Daddy are going out and never coming back. **(2)** I was mixed up with another baby at the hospital and they gave me to the wrong Mommy and Daddy. **(3)** My Daddy is going to kill me when he gets home. **(4)** My babysitter is going to kill me before my Mommy gets home. **(5)** My teddybear's Mommy is going to kill me for taking her baby.

If you have allotted yourself too much time or too much gasoline, you have been a poor sport and will create no anxiety. If you have allotted yourself too *little* time or gas, you have made missing the plane inevitable and have removed the fun of the chase.

But if you have planned this exercise with a reasonable amount of care, you will have one full hour of glorious Frenzy and Self-Torture—a sixty-minute slice of Total Personal Misery.

Quiz on Negative Thinking

Question: Which of the following sports are safe and which are dangerous?

- ☐ (a) Fishing
- ☐ (b) Sky-diving
- ☐ (c) Checkers
- ☐ (d) Golf
- ☐ (e) Tiddledywinks
- ☐ (f) Swimming
- ☐ (g) Ping-Pong
- ☐ (h) Hunting
- ☐ (i) Pitching horseshoes

Answers:

(a) Dangerous. A crazed giant turtle could attack you and try to pull you into his shell.

(b) Dangerous. Just as you are about to dive, you could trip, fall backwards into the plane and smack your head.

(c) Dangerous. In executing a quadruple jump across the board you could fall off your chair and break a rib.

(d) Dangerous. You could sink in quicksand while retrieving a ball from a sand trap.

(e) Dangerous. A tiddledy could ricochet off the wall and put out your eye, or it could become permanently lodged under your thumbnail.

(f) Dangerous. A seagull could drop a heavy clam on you and crush your head.

(g) Dangerous. A ping-pong ball could fly into your throat while your mouth was open and choke you to death.

(h) Dangerous. You could be sexually assaulted by a love-starved moose.

(i) Dangerous. You could pick up hoof-and-mouth disease from an unsterile horseshoe.

Chapter 2: Seven Classic
Misery-Making Situations

You have been exposed to most of the following classic Misery-Making Situations before, but because you hadn't yet read this book it is doubtful that you were able to derive any more than superficial pain from them.

As you read through these situations now, armed with the techniques we have taught you thus far, see how many of your own subjective, personalized worries you can add to the basic list, and how many you are able to turn into First-Class Anxieties.

Situation #1: Basic Worries About Noises in the Night

During the night, as heat escapes from the walls of your home and the various joints and braces and timbers contract and then later on during the hours preceding dawn as these

FIG. IV: VISUAL AID TO INTERPRETATION OF NOISES IN NIGHT

Keep this diagram next to your bed. When you hear any of the following noises during the night, match them with the corresponding guide numbers in the illustration above in order to interpret them imaginatively.

(1) wind in chimney; (2) branches of tree brushing against house; (3) beams in attic contracting; (4) air currents rustling drapery; (5) moth in light fixture; (6) steam escaping from radiator; (7) shrinking timbers in basement; 8) motor of deepfreeze; (9) dripping faucet.

same joints and braces and timbers expand, you are apt to hear a number of curious creaking noises.

You should be able to convince yourself these noises are one or more of the following:

(1)   A hideous-looking criminal who is going to rob you and stab you.

(2)   A hideous-looking crazy-person just escaped from an insane asylum who is going to stab you and rape you.

(3)   A hideous-looking ghoul, vampire, zombie or creature from another planet who is going to rape you and kill you.

(4)   A hideous-looking man from the Bureau of Internal Revenue who is going to find discrepancies in your tax return.

Situation #2: Basic Worries About Giving and Receiving Gifts

When buying a gift for somebody, worry about the following:

(1)   They already have one.

(2)   Not only do they already have one, but they hate it.

(3)   The gift they're getting me will be much more expensive and mine will look cheap next to theirs.

(4)   They're not getting me anything at all.

(5) They'll get me something I already have, or something I hate, and when I go to the store to return it, I'll run into them at the exchange counter.

Situation #3: Basic Worries About Waiting

What to think about while waiting for the results of a job interview:
(1) I asked for too much money.
(2) I asked for little money.
(3) I appeared too eager.
(4) I didn't appear eager enough.
(5) I don't deserve such a good job.

What to think about while waiting for someone who's late for an appointment:
(1) I'm waiting in the wrong place.
(2) An emergency came up at the last minute, they can't make it, and they don't know how to reach me.
(3) They probably aren't coming. They probably never intended to come.
(4) Everybody who passes by knows how long I've been waiting and is laughing at me.
(5) I was a little late myself and they've already been here and gone.

(For further guidance in this area, consult the section *Waiting for a Phone Call* in Chapter 5.)

Situation #4: Basic Worries About Vacations

When on vacation in your own country:

(1) Picture the door you probably forgot to lock and all the people who have wandered into your living room and are having an orgy.

(2) Picture the faucet you probably forgot to turn off and the water as it cascades over the sides of the sink or tub, seeping out into the rest of the house, drowning your carpets, then your furniture, then your clothes, and finally bursting out of your windows and onto the street.

(3) Picture the lights or the stove you probably forgot to turn off, the overheating of electrical circuits or the build-up of gas, and the inevitable flaming holocaust and explosion.

(4) Picture your doorstep as the milk delivery you probably forgot to cancel accumulates and quietly curdles into fourteen quarts of warm cottage cheese.

(5) Picture the place you work and everything going to hell in your absence.

(6) Picture the place you work and everything going more smoothly than ever in your absence.

FIG. V.: BASIC WORRY FOR TRAVELERS ABROAD

Shown are two taxi routes (solid line and broken line) from hotel (**H**) to restaurant (**R**). Which is the route for residents of the country? Which route will *you* be taken on?

When on vacation in a foreign country concentrate on the following ideas:

(1) Somebody is waiting to snatch my cameras.

(2) Somebody has been rifling my suitcase.

(3) Did I have seven pieces of luggage *including* or *not* including the camera bag?

(4) I can't understand what they're saying but they're obviously making fun of me.

(5) The minute they realized I was an American the price went up. Also, I left a tip and the service was probably included.

(6) The taxi driver is taking a circuitous route and the place I am going to is probably just around the corner.

(7) I feel dizzy, which means I'm probably sick, because although I haven't been drinking the water I *have* been brushing my teeth with it, and I am coming down with a strange foreign disease which the doctor, who won't understand English, will diagnose incorrectly and I'll die all alone in a strange country.

(8) The swarthy-looking man standing next to me outside the American Embassy is an Arab terrorist. He has an Uzi machine gun in his attaché case and is wearing a bomb made of *plastique* under his coat. He is prepared to die for his ideals and take me with him.

Situation #5: Basic Worries About Dinner Parties

If it is you who are entertaining:

Worry that nobody you invited will come, that there'll be too little food, that there'll be too *much* food, that they won't *like* the food, that nobody will mix, that they'll break your good glassware, that they'll leave cigarette burns in the upholstery, that they'll spill things on the carpet, that they'll steal something, or that they'll step on your dog or cat or child.

If you're going to someone else's house:

Worry that you won't remember the names of people you've met before, that people you've met before won't remember *your* name, that nobody will talk to you, that you'll spill something or break something, that you won't like what's being served or you'll be allergic to it or it will compromise your diet and you'll either have to insult the hostess by not eating it or else eat it and be sick afterwards.

Special thoughts for the latter part of the evening:

If you're at someone else's house, alternate between thinking (1) that they wish you'd leave already and (2) that they'd be terribly hurt if you left so soon. Tell them it's time you were going and see if they coax you to stay.

If you're the host, when a guest says it's time he was

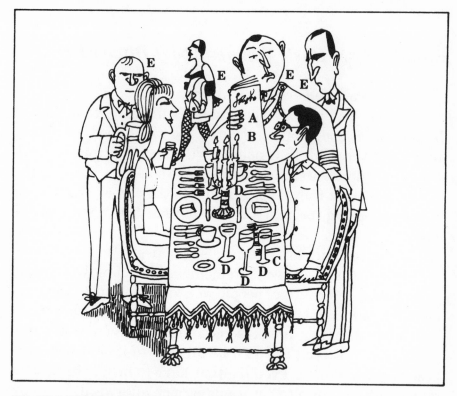

FIG. VI: BASIC WORRIES ABOUT DINING OUT

(A) The prices on the menu will be too high and you'll be embarrassed to get up and leave; **(B)** the dishes on the menu will be in a language you don't understand and you'll feel foolish asking for translations; **(C)** you won't know which fork to use; **(D)** you'll inadvertently knock over a glass and spill the contents all over or upset the candelabra and set your date on fire; **(E)** by tipping the person who gives you your coat and not the one who took it from you, or by tipping the waiter and not the captain, or by tipping the waiter and the captain but not the headwaiter, or by tipping all of the preceding too little or too much or by tipping someone you're not supposed to, you will prove yourself a clod.

going—even if it's possible he's saying this in hopes you'll coax him to stay—fear he wants to leave because he's bored and don't coax him.

Situation #6: Basic Worries About Minor Infractions of the Law

Each time you do something illegal—like running a red light or dropping litter on the street or jaywalking or sneaking into a show or double-parking or not using your seatbelt or smoking pot or not declaring purchases to Customs officials or cheating on your income tax—think as follows:

(1) Everybody knows. Everybody is looking at me.

(2) I'll be caught. Millions of people do it all the time, but *me* they'll catch.

(3) The story will be in all the papers and will go into the permanent computer files they keep on everybody, and every prospective employer or credit manager or policeman in the world will know me on sight for the rest of my life.

Situation #7: Basic Worries About Pregnancy and Natural Childbirth*

Pregnancy and childbirth are ideal circumstances in which to torture yourself. Fears about the pain and dangers of childbirth and birth defects potentially satisfy all previously stated requirements for converting fears into 3-Dimensional Worries and 3-Dimensional Worries into First-Class Anxieties. No matter what you do, you're just going to have to wait nine months until you can find out if your fears were justified.

It is appropriate to worry about the health of your fetus if you have exposed it to alcoholic beverages; beverages containing caffeine, like coffee, tea, Coca-Cola, or Pepsi-Cola; aspirin or any other prescription or nonprescription drug;

---

* Pregnancy and childbirth should probably not even be in this section. It should probably be in Section II: Methods to Misery with Others, because most women who get pregnant tend not to do so alone but with a husband or a close friend of some kind. But we thought it belonged here in Section I: Methods to Misery Alone—shortly after you learned about 3-Dimensional Worries and First-Class Anxieties. Do you think we were wrong? Would you like us to change it? Unfortunately, now it's too late. But maybe we'll fix it for the next edition— in 2008.

recreational drugs such as marijuana or cocaine; x-rays at the doctor or dentist; PCB-contaminated fish, EDB-laced citrus fruits and grains, or additive-laden groceries, or to the cumulative effects of drinking the water and breathing the air in any moderately big city.

"But," you say, "I have been scrupulously careful. Since the moment I learned I was pregnant, I have totally abstained from liquor, wine, beer, coffee, tea, Coke, Pepsi, aspirin, prescription drugs, nonprescription drugs, marijuana, cocaine, x-rays, fish, citrus fruits, grains, groceries, drinking water, and breathing air."

All well and good, but what about the period *before* you found out you were pregnant? Might you have accidentally exposed the fetus to any spermicides? Might you have sipped a Harvey Wallbanger or popped a couple of Excedrins?

"No," you persist, "I have had none of those, and I drink only decaffeinated coffee."

Perhaps you didn't know that even decaffeinated coffee has caffeine. Perhaps you didn't know that there is new medical evidence to suggest that some decaffeinated beverages might be even more dangerous than caffeinated ones: some decaffeinating processes use formaldehyde, which leaves a residue on the coffee beans; some use methylene chloride, which is an animal carcinogen.

Since the authors of this book are both cat lovers, there

is one worry that we would like to pass along to pregnant people who own cats: toxoplasmosis.

Toxoplasmosis is caused by a microscopic protozoan named *Toxoplasma gondii* and is transmitted by contact with infected cat poop. People who contract the disease never know they have it, but a pregnant woman who catches it during the first three months of pregnancy has a 17 percent chance of infecting her fetus. Of this 17 percent, 80 percent of the infected fetuses will be stillborn or show severe manifestations of disease such as abnormally large heads, abnormally small heads, blindness, convulsions, or cerebral calcifications.

What can you do to make sure your cats don't have toxoplasmosis? Well, you can collect their poop in an empty yogurt container and keep it in the refrigerator till you can take it to the vet to be lab tested, hoping nobody in your house opens the container, anticipating yogurt.

Of course, stool samples may show nothing, and your cats may still be infected. And if you have more than one cat, how will you ever know whose poop you're saving unless you're actually there when it's pooped? Standing guard over a litter box for several hours in hopes of catching a cat pooping is surely an activity worthy of this book.

A more reliable method—not only for the cats, but for

pregnant moms—is the blood test. Cats love blood tests even more than do pregnant moms, and imagine their delight to learn that not one but *two* of them are required, a few weeks apart.

Even then, you can never be certain. All you can determine is whether the pregnant mom and the cats have toxoplasmosis *antibodies* in their blood, and whether the level went up or down or stayed the same between tests. The worst possible scenario is for the pregnant mom to have no antibodies and for the cats to have rising antibodies.

So what do you do, give your cats away for nine months? What would they think was happening to them? Would they even know you when you came to get them back? Who would take cats for nine months? No, better to keep them and try to make sure the pregnant mom never changes the cat litter and never comes in contact with cat poop, and then spend nine months worrying about babies with abnormally large or small heads.

There are, of course, a couple of ways to check the condition of your fetus during pregnancy—sonograms and amniocentesis. But sonograms don't really give you much information about birth defects, and amniocentesis—which involves inserting a hypodermic needle into the mother's belly and into the fetus itself and withdrawing fluid—is only good for detecting Down's syndrome. Worse than that, amniocentesis is a fairly dangerous proposition and could damage or even kill the fetus.

So there really isn't anything to be done after all but wait. Here are some things to worry about while you're waiting:

(1) Worry that someone with a cold or a virus or the flu will give it to you while you're pregnant and, because you are unable to take any medicines for fear of endangering the fetus, you will be sick for the entire nine months.

(2) Worry about the unbearable, excruciating, and indescribable pain of natural childbirth, which—let's face it— is hardly going to disappear because of any kind of Lamaze rhythmic breathing, no matter how ridiculous you sound while you're doing it.

(3) If you should choose to concede defeat and lessen the pain of childbirth with epidural anesthesia—which is an injection into the base of your spine: (a) worry that the anesthetic will damage the baby; (b) worry that the needle will miss the incredibly tiny target area it has to hit and will cause a horrendously painful spinal tap; (c) worry that they will inject the wrong fluid, as they did with a pregnant woman in Albany, N.Y., on March 8, 1985, which left her paralyzed and breathing only with the aid of a respirator. (The National Center for Health Statistics in Bethesda, Md.,

reports that more than 2,000 patients a year die as a result of medical accidents.)

(4) Worry that your baby will accidentally be switched in the hospital by a moronic nurse and brought up by another set of parents, and you will only discover the switch after several years, by which time you will be too attached to the wrong baby to give him up, and the other parents will be too attached to *your* baby to give him up, and they will have to make a TV miniseries about you.

(5) Worry where the hell you're ever going to come up with the $800,000 or so that it will cost you to bring this baby up and send it to college.

Situation #8: Basic Worries About Fitness, Exercise and Dieting

If you're in your thirties or older, you have probably been giving a little thought to putting off as long as possible the moment when you begin hobbling about in a walker with saliva dribbling down your chin. To this end, you may have changed your diet and started upon some program of regular aerobic exercise.

Congratulations! You are doing a wise and healthy thing. And don't even *think* about the fact that Adelle Davis, one of the world's foremost diet experts, who maintained that any disease could be prevented by proper diet, died on May 31, 1974, of bone cancer.

And don't think about the fact that Jim Fixx—certainly one of the world's foremost runners and advocates of running as a means of strengthening the heart and preventing coronary heart disease, who ran ten miles every single day, no matter what—suffered a fatal heart attack on July 20, 1984, at the age of 52, while running.

Exercise can be quite healthy, provided: (a) you don't exceed your aerobic training range; (b) you don't neglect to cool down after strenuous exercise and cause your blood to pool below your waist and drain from your heart and brain and cause cardiac arrest; (c) you don't drop a dumbbell on your foot and crush it; (d) you don't catch athlete's foot in the gym locker room.

Diet is terribly important too. You will certainly want to cut out hamburgers, hot dogs, roast beef, steaks, lamb, pork, bacon, sausage, eggs, olives, peanut butter, anything made with white flour, anything made with white rice, anything made with butter, anything made with salt, and anything made with refined sugar, like cake, ice cream, cookies, candy, Fudgesicles, Devil Dogs, or Hostess Twinkies.

A man named Dan White went berserk after eating Twinkies and killed San Francisco's Mayor Mosconi and his associate Harvey Milk. The probability is high that in most public places you visit, someone nearby has recently ingested at least one Twinkie and could go berserk and kill you.

Be wary of Alzheimer's disease. It begins with forgetfulness and minor mental confusion and progresses to difficulty in coping with life's everyday activities, like dressing and undressing oneself, going to the toilet, recognizing loved ones, and recognizing your own face in the mirror. People who get Alzheimer's may live from two to twenty years, but usually only five to eight, and it's incurable. Any word or name you can't remember might just be the first symptom of . . . uh, whatever it is.

Brood about what it's going to be like to grow old in a society that worships youth. Compare yourself to the younger people you meet or see in movies and on TV and in commercials and wonder if anybody still finds you physically attractive.

Look for the telltale signs that you are already sliding downhill: gray hairs, a bald spot, failing eyesight, bags under your eyes, crow's feet, turkey neck, a spare tire around your middle, sagging breasts and buttocks, and liver spots. Consider that, as old as you think you look now, this is the youngest that you will ever look again—some day you'll wish you looked this good.

Read the obituaries. Note the ages at which most people die. Figure out how many summers you have left, how many

Christmases, how many birthdays. Console yourself by looking around and noticing everybody who is older than you and still ambulatory. Let each birthday be a slap in the face. Begin brooding about it on your half-birthday. Picture your birthday cake collapsing from the weight of the candles.

Brood about how fast life goes by, about all the things you planned to do that you never will, and about all the places to which you will never travel. Brood about how little money you put away for your old age, about how deeply in debt you are, and about how horrible it would be if you became seriously ill and they had to wheel your hospital bed out into the street because you couldn't afford to pay your bills. Hum the folk song, "You load sixteen tons and what do you get, you get another day older and deeper in debt. . . ."

Worry about how many of your brain cells have already died. Worry that you will eventually lose the ability to take care of yourself, that you'll be a burden to your family, an object of pity, and a laughingstock. Worry that you'll get senile and become a vegetable on a life support system and that nobody will ever have the guts to pull the plug.

Situation #9: Basic Worries About Flying

We strongly recommend flying on commercial airlines for two important reasons.

FIG. VII: WORRYING ABOUT MINOR INFRACTIONS OF THE LAW

You are passing through Customs with an undeclared purchase in your suitcase. Anticipate the reaction of each person in line with you when your crime is exposed.

First, it is an excellent opportunity for you as a novice to practice your Anxiety-Creating Techniques, since any fear of crashing will instantly fulfill all requirements for a 3-Dimensional Worry (or perhaps even a First-Class Anxiety), as outlined in Chapter 1.

Second, never will you be in a better position to meet so many fellow masochists at a single time, since everybody who travels by plane is terrified of flying, and since everybody on your plane (unless you spot handcuffs or a revolver somewhere in the cabin) has rejected the idea of a safer means of transportation and is present purely by choice.

The basic anxiety, from the moment you phone in your reservation up until the moment you board, is: Whatever plane you have reservations on is the one that's going to crash, and the only way to avoid certain doom is to change your reservation to another plane—which, of course, you feel too sheepish to do. (If you actually do have enough guts to switch to another plane, the anxiety then becomes: It's not the plane you changed *from* but the you changed *to* that is going to crash.)

The basic anxiety once you're on the plane, after the big steel door has been locked but before the plane actually leaves the ground is: "The swarthy-looking man sitting next to me is an Arab terrorist. He has an Uzi machine gun in his attaché case and is wearing a bomb made of *plastique* under his coat. He is prepared to die for his ideals and take me with him."

In flight, and in some cases just prior to boarding, you will be subjected to a number of oblique and ominous messages by the personnel of the airline. In order to properly understand and exploit these messages you will need to translate them into Plain Talk. The sample below should aid you in making such translations.

WHAT THEY SAY	WHAT THEY MEAN
(1) Ladies and gentlemen, there will be a slight delay in boarding the aircraft due to a few minor difficulties.	(1) One of our wings was about to fall off and the crew needs time to Scotch-tape it back to the fuselage.
(2) Kindly fasten your seat belts and observe the No Smoking signs, as we are about to encounter some minor turbulence.	(2) The tape broke and the wing fell off.
(3) If you look out of the windows to your left, you should be able to see the outskirts of Indianapolis.	(3) It was the *right* wing that fell off.

(4) We'll be landing in another eight to ten minutes, ladies and gentlemen, so before we get too busy up here I'd like to say, on behalf of myself and our crew, that we've enjoyed having you aboard this flight.

(4) It takes a little time for the crew to strap on parachutes and bail out.

Nine Hideous New Facts on Flying for Advanced Practitioners

First we want to tell you nine ghastly true things about commercial flying that you probably didn't know. Then we'll tell you why we're telling you. Here we go:

(1) On DC-10s, the aft cargo door has an annoying habit of blowing off and the pylons that attach the engines to the wings sometimes crack and break, which occasionally causes the engines to land somewhat sooner than the rest of the plane.

(2) Although it's against federal regulations, many pilots still booze it up on the sly during flights. One airline pilot commented recently: "Any flight where you don't have a near miss is a dull flight."

(3) At Los Angeles International Airport, planes take

off and land in opposite directions on parallel runways, which one pilot called "a 200-mile-per-hour game of Chicken."

(4)   The obsolete computers that keep track of aircraft taking off and landing are always going on the fritz, leaving air traffic controllers staring at blank scopes.

(5)   A jumbo jet uses about $1,850 worth of kerosene every hour, but penny-pinching airlines allot the smallest possible amount of fuel on board because it *takes* fuel to *carry* fuel. If you have to spend awhile stacked up in a holding pattern or you get diverted to another airport, you have an excellent chance of flaming out and going down without fuel. (Fuel gauges on airliners can be off by several thousand pounds.)

(6)   In a forced landing, your seatbelt will rupture your spleen and fracture your pelvic saddle. Your seat is stressed to nine Gs, which sounds swell until you learn that nine Gs is less than the minimum requirement for cars.

(7)   Your floatable seat cushion is considered by the Coast Guard to be unsuitable for nonswimmers and children. If you have a life vest under your seat you'll find it hard to extract, unpack, put on, and inflate, and it won't keep your head above water. Even trained crew members are hazy about how to use them.

(8)   If your plane lands in water and it doesn't break up

on impact it will float anywhere from eleven seconds to four days. A Coast Guard helicopter can pick up only twenty people from the water under ideal conditions. The rest will freeze or drown.

(9) In case you think that economics will eventually force the industry to give in and make flying safer, we've been assured that the airlines could triple the rate at which they now crash planes and feel no pain financially. Recently National Airlines crashed a 727 into Florida's Escambia Bay. National realized an after-tax profit of $1,500,000 from the disaster due to excess insurance coverage on the plane. Ten days after the crash, National issued a press release explaining that the profit came from "the involuntary conversion of a 727 aircraft."

Aren't you glad we told you all those things? Is it going to make you stop flying and start taking trains? Is it going to tempt you to make that next business trip from Bangor, Maine to Waco, Texas, in your Chevy? Not on your life it isn't.

You'll still keep on flying, even during severe electrical storms, even if you see the pilot stagger into the cockpit clutching a brown paper bag with a bottle in it, and even during pilots' strikes when the planes are being flown by baggage handlers.

And if you ever lose an engine and come down on foam

at J.F.K. Airport, with fire vehicles and guys in asbestos suits standing by to extinguish you, and you promise God you'll never fly again if only He will let you live this one time, that promise will be good for about sixteen hours, tops.

You know why? Because you're a masochist and because flying is so fast and so easy, and the alternatives are so *inconvenient,* that's why. You dread inconvenience even more than going down as numerous pieces of flaming wreckage at J.F.K.

Despite all that we know about the horrors of airline safety, we are consistently assured that flying is, statistically, safer than driving. It is hard to see how that could be possible. Maybe what they mean to say is, flying is, statistically, safer than driving ninety miles an hour against traffic with your trousers over your ears.

Quiz

Question #1: Is the safest seat on a plane:
- ☐ (a) in front of the engines on a jet and behind them on a propellor aircraft?
- ☐ (b) behind the engines on a jet and in front of them on a propellor aircraft?
- ☐ (c) nearest the wing?
- ☐ (d) where the stewardesses sit?

Answer: There *is* no safe seat on a plane.

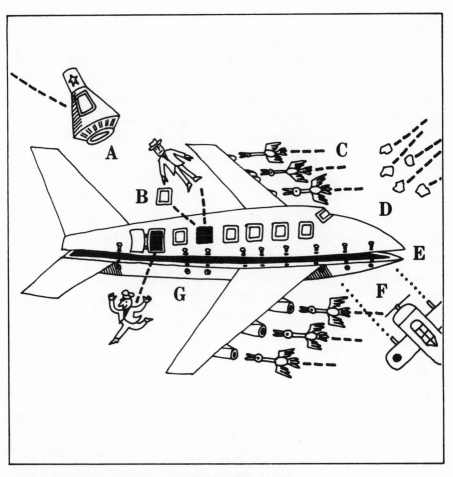

FIG. VIII: POSSIBILITIES TO CONSIDER WHILE FLYING

(A) Re-entering space capsule could collide with plane; **(B)** poorly sealed window could pop out, sucking you through opening; **(C)** six wild geese could simultaneously enter and clog jets; **(D)** sudden meteorite shower could puncture fuselage; **(E)** excessive vibration could loosen bolts holding top and bottom halves of plane together; **(F)** plane could be shot down by die-hard WW II kamikaze pilot; **(G)** disturbed pilot could leap from plane in fit of pique.

Question #2:   When you reach your destination, should you:
- ☐ (a)   immediately double your flight insurance for the return trip?
- ☐ (b)   immediately cancel your return-trip ticket and transfer to a train or boat?
- ☐ (c)   try to figure out whether, to avoid a return trip on *any* form of potentially hazardous transportation, you couldn't just settle in the city where you've landed?

Answer: What makes you think you're *going* to reach your destination?

Chapter 3: Misery About the Past, the Present and the Future

Optimum Brooding Conditions

If you are serious about making yourself miserable, you will meet no greater foe than constructive activity, no greater friend than absolute inactivity.

Inactivity is the fertile ground in which flourish the seeds of despair and self-pity. Doing nothing at all—sitting on an uncomfortable wooden chair and looking out the window or lying in bed staring at the ceiling—you are ideally situated to brood about all the bad breaks you've ever had, all the inadequacies you've ever noticed in your personality or appearance, and all the possibilities for misery in your past, your present and your future.

Is there a time, you may ask, a particularly propitious time to accomplish such brooding? There is indeed.

Sunday Afternoon

The best time of the week for brooding is the time of greatest inactivity—Sunday afternoon.

Monday through Friday aren't much good for brooding because then you are caught up in the busy schedule of work or study and you simply don't have the time. Besides, you are looking forward to The Weekend. All sorts of grand things could happen on The Weekend, and the closer it gets the less you're going to feel like brooding. (Late Friday afternoon is generally about the worst time of the week to get any serious brooding done.)

By Saturday morning you may be vaguely aware that Friday night wasn't as great as you hoped it would be, but you don't have much time to think about it even then because you have many errands to do before the stores close and, of course, you are still looking forward to the climax of The Weekend—Saturday Night.

By Sunday afternoon, however, it is all over. Hope is dead. There is nothing further to look forward to, except the gloomy prospect of Monday morning and another whole week of drudgery at a job or a school you detest. The Weekend—like your life—can at last be viewed in its correct perspective: one colossal letdown, one gigantic anticlimax. On Sunday afternoon you are free to ponder all the great times you felt sure lay ahead but which never quite materialized.

Yes, Sunday afternoon is a marvelous time for brooding. But as marvelous as Sunday afternoon is, there is another time which is even better.

Surely the best time of all for brooding and self-pity is that yearly intersection of past, present and future, that annual orgy of self-flagellation—New Year's Eve.

New Year's Eve

Hooray! Everything connected with New Year's Eve is ideally suited to misery. The moment Thanksgiving is over it is permissible to start dreading the arrival of the evening of December 31.

Some of the things you may look forward to are: (1) the inevitable impossibility of obtaining reservations at any good restaurant or show; (2) the prospect of being repeatedly jostled by drunken revelers or maimed by drunken drivers; (3) the humiliation of paying fifty to one hundred dollars per person for a glass of cheap champagne, an imitation TV dinner and two dimestore party favors.

If you're not married or otherwise attached, you are permitted the additional anxiety that you'll end up with a date you'll be embarrassed to be seen with—or that you won't be able to get a date at all.

When the great night arrives, you can either: (1) deliberately ostracize yourself from your friends and be miserable alone, or (2) put on a funny paper hat and drink too much with the rest of the group, postponing your brooding till the following day, when you will have ample opportunity to regret your behavior and be sick.

Either way, the occasion will provide you with an abundance of rich Brooding Material—like all the things which you promised yourself last New Year's Eve you would accomplish in the year just ended, and like the fact that every year you get to look less and less like the little kid with the diaper and the banner across his chest and more and more like the old guy with the beard and the hourglass and the scythe.

So between New Year's Eves, Sunday afternoons and whatever additional time you can periodically set aside, you should manage to get a lot of good brooding done—provided, of course, that you can keep this precious time free of constructive activity.

Should you ever be tempted to undertake any type of constructive activity—like looking for a better job, meeting somebody of the opposite sex, taking up a hobby, entering a

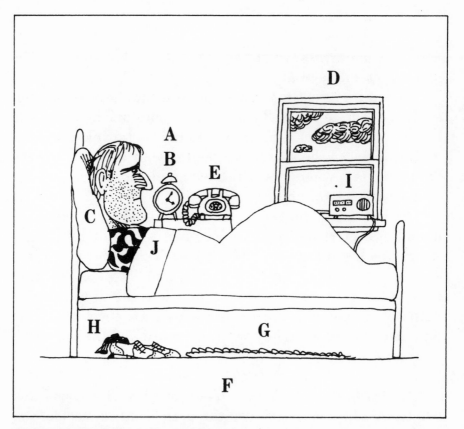

FIG. IX: REASONS FOR NOT GETTING OUT OF BED

(A) It's too early; (B) it's already too late; (C) you would have to shave; (D) weather might change; (E) phone might ring any minute; (F) it's warm under covers but floor is probably cold; (G) you might slip on rug and wrench your back; (H) you might not have any more clean socks; (I) important radio program is not yet over; (J) by pulling wrong foot out from under covers first you might get caught in sheets and strangle.

contest, going into business for yourself or getting out of bed to make breakfast—quickly refer to the following list. Read it aloud repeatedly, and persist until all temptation toward constructive activity has passed.

Seventeen Basic Pessimistic Philosophies

(1) I can't do it.
(2) I never could do anything right.
(3) I have the worst luck in the world.
(4) I don't have a chance, so why try?
(5) I'm all thumbs.
(6) I'd only get hurt.
(7) It would never work.
(8) It's not in the stars.
(9) It's never been done before.
(10) It's not who you are, it's who you know.
(11) It's too late now.
(12) It's later than you think. .
(13) You can't take it with you.
(14) What good could come of it?
(15) The piper must be paid.
(16) The wages of sin is death.
(17) The paths of glory lead but to the grave.

So what's the use? Whatever it is, you'd better forget

about it. You just couldn't handle it. You wouldn't know what to do. You wouldn't know what to say. You'd bungle it and everybody would laugh at you. Perhaps you could tackle it sometime in the future. Maybe you could try it after you've had a chance to prepare a little more. But not now. Better wait. Better postpone it. Better retreat.

Now that constructive activity is no longer a temptation, let's take a look at some of the things you can torture yourself about in your past, your present and your future.

How to Make Yourself Miserable About the Past

The secret of being truly miserable about the past lies in being able to regret everything you ever did and everything you ever failed to do, from the moment you were born right up to five minutes ago.

The following suggestions should get you started on your own personal list of regrets:

(1) I should have gotten married when I had the chance.
(2) I shouldn't have gotten married so young.
(3) I shouldn't have let them put whipped cream on my Jell-O.
(4) I should have held out for more money.
(5) I should have accepted his offer.

(6) I should have studied more in college and frolicked less.

(7) I should have studied less in college and frolicked more.

(8) I shouldn't have agreed to come here tonight.

(9) I should have taken along an umbrella.

(10) I shouldn't have dragged along an umbrella.

(11) I shouldn't have allowed myself to become involved.

(12) I should have waited till it went on sale.

(13) I should have just walked up and introduced myself.

(14) I should have told them exactly what I thought of them.

(15) I shouldn't have moved from New York to a city as culturally stagnant as Los Angeles.

(16) I shouldn't have moved from Los Angeles to a city as pushy and dirty and unfriendly as New York.

(17) I should have quit when I was ahead.

How to Make Yourself Miserable About the Present

If you aren't rich, famous, beautiful or talented, making yourself miserable about the present should be as easy for you as knowing whom and how to envy.

But if you *are* rich, famous, beautiful or talented, there's no need to feel left out. Making yourself miserable is no more difficult than knowing what to brood about.

In the following section we have provided you with Basic Brooding Material for all of the above-mentioned life situations. The thoughts presented, we hasten to point out, are not intended as a complete list but merely as a guide to the formation of your own Brooding Material. Obviously, the material you come up with yourself is going to be much more relevant and much deadlier than any we could suggest to you.

How to Make Yourself Miserable If You're Not a Rich Person:

(1) Brood about how rich people can buy all the nice things *you've* always dreamed of owning but could never afford; about how rich people can walk into a store and buy anything—any *silly* thing—any crazy, impulsive, totally *impractical* thing—just because they feel like it—*and not even have to ask the price.*

(2) Brood about how rich people never have to work if they don't feel like it. Thus they have time to do all the things *you* want to do but can't because you have to work for a living.

FIG X: CLASSIC UNGRASPED OPPORTUNITIES FOR MISERY ABOUT THE PAST

(**A**) You could have bought Los Angeles real estate before WW II; (**B**) you could have married the homely rich girl in your junior high school class; (**C**) you could have bought IBM stock in 1938; (**D**) you could have invented frozen food.

(3) Brood about how rich people can tell anyone they wish to go to hell.

How to Make Yourself Miserable If You ARE a Rich Person:

(1) Brood about all the great things you could have done with all the money you've paid in taxes if you had found some way to avoid paying it.

(2) Brood about all the people you have to pay just to help you hang on to what's left of your money.

(3) Brood about all the people who are charging you more for their services just because you're rich.

(4) Wonder whether your money is really working for you as well in the relatively safe place you've invested it now as it could be in a more speculative investment.

(5) Wonder whether your money really *is* safe where you have it invested now.

(6) Wonder whether you're living way beyond your means; whether you should cut expenses by giving up cabs for buses, fancy restaurants for lunch counters, etc., before you approach bankruptcy.

(7) Wonder whether the gifts you give to friends or to charities are really appreciated or taken for granted;

FIG. XI: SUPPLEMENTARY BROODING DIAGRAM FOR NON-RICH PERSONS

Study the above manifestations of comfortable income until you achieve either an upset stomach or a migraine headache.

whether the recipients feel you could have afforded a bit more.

(8) Wonder whether the people who are nice to you are only nice to you because of your money.

(9) Wonder whether those friends of yours who are less fortunate than you resent your money; whether you should begin to seek out a new circle of friends in a higher income bracket where you might feel less resented; whether you'd ever be accepted as a friend by anyone in a higher income bracket.

(10) Wonder whether being able to afford all the luxuries you've ever wanted is anticlimactic; whether there's anything left in life to look forward to.

How to Make Yourself Miserable If You're Not a Famous Person:

(1) Brood about how famous people can get away with anything—like never needing to wait in line; like being able to get tickets at the last minute for sold-out performances; like being allowed to walk into an expensive restaurant without a tie or a jacket on if they're a man, or with pants on if they're a lady—because the rules for un-famous people don't apply to famous people.

(2) Brood about how famous people lead such glamor-

ous, exciting lives, and how all famous people know all other famous people, and how everybody is always falling all over themselves to invite famous people to parties.

(3) Brood about how nobody ever forgets a famous person's name.

How to Make Yourself Miserable If You ARE a Famous Person:

(1) Brood about the privacy you no longer have—about being mobbed for autographs everywhere you go, even when you're eating in a restaurant or shopping, and how, as a result, you're no longer free to go to places that un-famous people go to all the time.

(2) Brood about how everybody keeps asking you the same questions about your life and your work and about how you have no right to get angry with them because you have to be nice to everyone—even to people who are not nice themselves—because they're your public, they are the ones who put you where you are and they are the ones who are keeping you there.

(3) Brood about how, since you are public property, all your personal problems are fair game for the press, and how even if you don't *have* any personal problems the columnists will make some up for you.

(4) Brood about how you are criticized for saying or doing, or for failing to say or do, things which un-famous people get away with all the time.

(5) Brood about how you have to go out of your way to prove to old friends that you haven't changed and are still the same lovable old you.

(6) Brood about the fact that the minute you're no longer on top you're a has-been; about all the young comers out there who are at this very minute training to replace you.

(7) Wonder whether you deserve to be famous at all.

How to Make Yourself Miserable If You're Not a Beautiful Person:

(1) Brood about how everybody likes beautiful people, and how they're a lot nicer to beautiful people than to un-beautiful people.

(2) Brood about how beautiful people can wear all the new styles and look absolutely marvelous in them, or how they can just throw on jeans and a sweater—scruffy things *you* wouldn't dare to wear in public—and look just as great.

(3) Brood about how much confidence beautiful people have, and about how beautiful people find jobs and love and marriage so much more easily than un-beautiful people do.

How to Make Yourself Miserable If You ARE a Beautiful Person:

(1) Brood about how much more care you have to take in keeping up your appearance than un-beautiful people do, about how much more you worry over blemishes, wrinkles, gray hair and calories.

(2) Brood about how people tend to overlook your other qualities—intelligence, sensitivity, talent, etc.—because they consider you a decorative object rather than a person.

(3) Brood about how quickly and easily looks are lost, and about how you'll feel worse after they're lost than if you never had them.

(4) Brood about how, since you've been lazy in developing your other qualities, you'll have nothing left at all when your looks are gone.

How to Make Yourself Miserable If You're Not a Talented Person:

(1) Brood about how everybody is always telling talented people how great they are and how great their work is.

(2) Brood about how talented people have the satisfaction of being involved with something creative—something more noble and enduring than the world of commerce; about

how the work that talented people do lives on after them, so they have a permanent place in posterity.

(3) Brood about how easily talented people can become rich people or famous people if they want to.

How to Make Yourself Miserable If You ARE a Talented Person:

(1) Brood about how, when you go to see the work of somebody in your own field, you're either so critical you have a terrible time, or else you're so envious you feel even worse.

(2) Brood about how you're fair game for critics who have no talent themselves.

(3) Brood about how, just when you seem to be getting somewhere in a certain circle, you are always pushed to compete in a bigger circle where your accomplishments look smaller and where the competition is much tougher.

(4) Brood about how, if you haven't been successful yet, your confidence runs out more and more with each failure; about how, if you *have* achieved success, you're only as good as your last effort, and you have to keep topping yourself to stay on top.

(5) Wonder whether you're losing your talent.

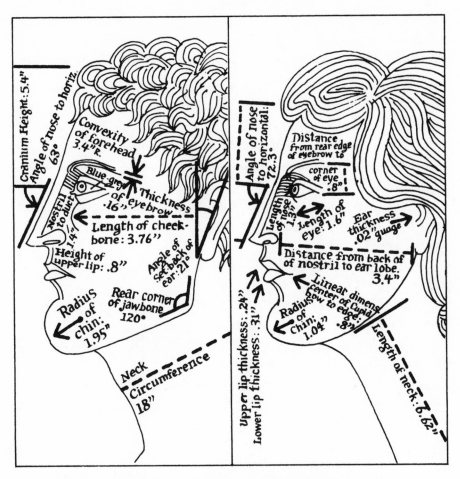

FIG. XII: FACIAL DIMENSIONS OF NORMAL MAN AND WOMAN

Compare the above measurements with your own or with those of a prospective lovemate. Any variation from the norm, no matter how slight, is a defect. Should you discover no defects, refer to the section *How to Make Yourself Miserable If You ARE a Beautiful Person.*

How to Make Yourself Miserable About the Future

Whether or not you can manage to remain miserable in the future is going to depend upon your ability to master two vital concepts:

(1) *Refuse to accept what cannot be changed.*

(2) *Establish unrealistic goals.*

What not to accept:

(1) Don't ever accept your age, or your weight, or your height, or your face, or your ethnic group, or your socioeconomic level.

(2) Don't ever acknowledge the fact that you make mistakes.

(3) Don't ever accept the possibility of failure, and don't ever prepare for it with alternative plans.

(4) Don't ever accept the fact that most people will never realize how great you are.

(5) Don't ever believe that the things other people have which you've always thought would make *you* happy aren't making *them* happy either.

What goals to establish:

(1) Find the perfect mate.

(2) Find the perfect job.

(3) Write the Great American Novel.

(4) Get even with the phone company.

Twenty-six-year-old patent office clerk, A. Einstein, formulated theory of relativity.

Swedish singer, Jenny Lind, was so popular that men paid $653.00 per seat to see her.

Youthful piano player, W. A. Mozart, had already composed his first symphony and three sets of sonatas by the age of eight.

Civil servant, Abdullah al-Salim of Kuwait, receives a salary of $7,280,-000 per week. Every two hours and forty minutes he earns the equivalent of the average American's lifetime income.

FIG. XIII: AID TO EVALUATING YOUR ACCOMPLISHMENTS

Compare yourself with these four ordinary people who were chosen at random.

(5) Develop a foolproof system to beat the horses, or the wheel at Las Vegas, or the stock market.

(6) Fight City Hall, and win.

(7) Get revenge for every injustice you've ever had to put up with in your entire life.

(8) Never be unrealistic again.

Exercise: Twenty-six Masochistic Activities for the Beginner

(1) Make a list of all the people you know who are younger than you and more successful.

(2) Make a list of all the things you nearly had but somehow blew.

(3) Make a list of all the great things you can't do anymore.

(4) Write a letter to somebody, mail it, and then figure out which part could be most easily misunderstood.

(5) Schedule your next nonessential drive downtown to coincide with a peak traffic hour.

(6) Schedule a Labor Day Weekend excursion without making advance reservations.

(7) Schedule a trip to New York in August or February. If you already live in New York, go to Philadelphia in August and to Chicago in February.

(8) Make it your business to see the next Steven Spielberg movie the night it opens.

(9) Buy a stock, check the market quotation every day in the paper, and every time it goes down figure out exactly how much money you lost.

(10) Using the tip of your tongue, see how long it takes you to make your gums bleed.

(11) Get yourself a medical book, copy down the symptoms of ten fatal diseases, and see how many you already have.

(12) If you're a young woman, ask the lady behind the cosmetics counter what to do about your face. Or take a scissors and cut off your nice long hair.

(13) Go to the beach and compare your body with anyone who has a very good build.

(14) Go to the bathroom in someone else's house and wonder if they can hear you.

(15) After leaving a room full of people, try to imagine what they might be saying about you.

(16) Spend one hour a week wondering whether you tip too little and everybody thinks you're cheap, or whether you tip too much and everybody thinks you're a sucker.

(17) Make a list of people you frequently have drinks or lunches with and figure out how many more times you've picked up the check than they have. Or else make a list of

everybody who owes you a small amount of money and who has obviously forgotten about it, and try to figure out how to get it back without seeming petty.

(18) Anytime you see something on sale that you already own, check the price to see how much you overpaid when you bought yours.

(19) Buy any brand of drug or food that in the past has been laced with cyanide or ground glass, like Tylenol, Gerber baby foods, Jell-O, or Chlor-a-septic mouthwash, as a show of support for the victimized manufacturer. Then keep the product on your shelf for months, vacillating about whether it's safe to use, even though it wasn't from one of the recalled lot numbers. Never use it, never return it, and never throw it away.

(20) If you work on a computer or word processor, worry (a) that somebody could leave your floppy discs next to a giant magnet or a set of stereo speakers and totally erase them; (b) that low frequency radiation from your video monitor is mutating your cells into malignancy; (c) that whenever you program your computer inaccurately and it flashes you signals like "Bad Command," "Command Ignored," or "Fatal Error," the machine thinks you're stupid and laughs about you behind your modem to other computers, like the cash machine at your bank.

(21) Imagine that some kid with a random access number is going to punch into your checking account through his P.C. and withdraw all your money.

(22) Think about how easy it would be for somebody to start a nuclear war by mistake or while they're stoned. Imagine that this nuclear holocaust will fragment the earth and cause the galaxy to be your grave. Or worse, imagine that you'll survive the nuclear holocaust and in the nuclear winter that follows, you won't be able to find any arugula, radicchio, or sun-dried tomatoes.

(23) Worry that you could choke to death in a little out-of-the-way restaurant where no one knows the Heimlich maneuver.

(24) If you have an insurance policy or a credit card, brood upon the fact that somewhere there is a file on you containing the most intimate and embarrassing information imaginable, which any governmental agency, private corporation, or anyone except you can have access to. It was compiled by sleazy so-called research firms who sold your bio for $1.50 and didn't have the time or interest to even get the details right, and this information is eventually going to get you refused for medical coverage or life insurance or a mortgage, or get you blackmailed or arrested or all of the foregoing. And when it happens, nobody is going to tell you why.

(25) If you like sushi, worry about the parasites it is now said to contain, parasites which reportedly attack Westerners and leave Asians alone.

(26) Worry that acid rain and air pollution are slowly killing you, that pesticides and chemical wastes in your water are slowly killing you, that cigarette smoke is slowly killing you even if you don't smoke, that radioactive fallout from Chernobyl has already drifted over here and is silently mutating your cells, or that some drug-crazed kid put something in the salt shaker in the coffee shop where you're eating, which will cause you to go and get a Mohawk haircut with Day-glo orange and green streaks and try to start a hard-core rock group.

Exercise: Four Masochistic Activities for the Advanced Practitioner

(1) Let's assume you know a little about CPR. One day you see somebody lying on the sidewalk, unconscious. Would you give that person mouth-to-mouth resuscitation or just walk away?

What if the person were an unclean vagrant? What if it were an attractive person of the opposite sex? What if you had reason to suspect the person might be a carrier of AIDS? How do you feel about the fact that you would probably just walk away and let him die when you could have saved his life? What if it were *you* on the ground unconscious and *he* walked away?

(2)   Before opening any of your mail, check the return address and try to figure out if there is any conceivable reason why that person might be sending you a letter bomb.

When you tear open an envelope containing a letter bomb, you trigger a small spring-loaded detonator that sets off three ounces of *plastique,* which causes a violent explosion and sends a shower of fatal splinters into your body.

(3)   Figure out the maximum price you would pay a kidnapper for the safe return of your dog or cat or a beloved member of your family. Figure out the maximum amount you'd pay a surgeon to save that pet or family member's life. Then figure out what you'd do if the kidnapper or the surgeon needed more than that amount.

If your response is to raise the maximum figure, then *that* is your maximum figure, not the other one. Now figure out what you'd do if the kidnapper or the surgeon needed more than *that.*

(4)   Try to imagine what you'd do if you passed by a burning building and heard that a child was trapped inside. (Don't say you'd call the fire department. The fire department has already been called, and they have had a tragic collision with an oil truck on the way to the fire.)

Completion Test

Directions: Fill in the missing words. Then compare your answers with those at the bottom of the page.

    (1) A penny saved is a penny _____.

    (2) _____ and his money are soon parted.

    (3) Nothing ventured, nothing _____.

    (4) Not much money, oh but honey, ain't we got

_____.

Answers:

    (1) depreciated   (3) lost

    (2) Anybody   (4) debts

SECTION II:
Methods to Misery With Others

Chapter 4: How to Lose Friends and Alienate People

In Section I you learned how to make yourself miserable through the creation of anxieties. You will soon find that the mere creation of anxieties will cease to be an effective means of self-torture unless you are allowed to put these anxieties to practical use.

One of the most practical ways to utilize anxieties is as a means of getting people to reject you. Obviously, the more people you can get to dislike you, the more miserable you'll be. Employers, lovers, wives, husbands, friends, even casual acquaintances—all can be made to reject you by proper use of the techniques set forth below.

Before you are ready to tackle our actual Reject-Me

Techniques, however, you must first formulate for yourself a suitable Reject-Me Image.

How to Formulate a Reject-Me Image

Everything about you—your tone of voice, your posture, the way you enter a room—tells people who you are and how you want them to treat you.

Therefore, you must weed out of your image any appealing qualities that might encourage people to accept you.

In general, try to be as apologetic, boring, critical, complaining, impatient, irritable, jealous, nervous, suspicious and wishy-washy as prudence will allow.

Always hang back and wait to be coaxed to participate in a group activity when everybody else just joins in of his own accord.

Be sloppy about personal hygiene. Forget people's names. Nurse grudges. Sulk. Never do what anybody else wants to do. Take yourself very seriously. Be a bad sport. Be impossible to please. If anyone should act enthusiastic about anything, be a wet blanket.* When with a proud parent or pet-owner, confess your aversion to children or animals. Re-

---

* See *Basic Pessimistic Philosophies.*

member: *Sometimes you must first* APPEAR *to reject in order to be rejected.**

And now for the specifics.

The Reject-Me Posture

Stand facing a full-length mirror. Slowly let your chest collapse. Crane your neck forward and peer sideways out of the corner of your eye. Let your shoulders sag. Now pretend your are a turtle and, without uncraning your neck or unsagging your shoulders, try to pull your head down into your shell. This, when properly mastered, is the correct Reject-Me Posture.

Your walk should be a direct outgrowth of your posture —that is, a hesitant, suspicious, moving slouch. Or, to put it more graphically: *Learn to enter a room as though you expected at any moment to be struck in the face.*

The Reject-Me Tone of Voice

Your tone of voice should be indistinct and whiney, and it should come from your nose rather than from your dia-

---

* Caution: If you're too obvious about provoking a rejection you'll miss out on a lot of righteous indignation when it finally happens.

phragm. The following nostalgic phrases should aid you in cultivating the proper Reject-Me Tone of Voice:

(1) "I don't *wanna* play that game."
(2) "Gimme my ball, I'm going *home*."
(3) "That's not yours, that's *mine*."
(4) "Mommy, make him give it *back*."

The Dynamics of Rejection

Now that you have begun to develop your Reject-Me Image, you are no doubt eager to get out there in the field and get rejected. We applaud your enthusiasm, but a word of caution is in order.

Winning your first big rejection is not quite as easy as it looks. Why? Well, for one thing, all potential rejec*tors* are also potential rejec*tees*—which is to say that somebody you are counting on to reject you might just turn around and act as though you've already rejected *him*. Thus:

YOU: "Hello. I'm awfully sorry—I guess I'm phoning at a bad time, aren't I?"

HE: "Why, hello. No, not at all. As a matter of fact, I'm a little hurt that you haven't called before this."

To prevent this type of embarrassing and unsatisfying occurrence,* and to guarantee you your all-important rejection, you will need to have a thorough grasp of the Dynamics of Rejection. You will need to know how to select a Promising Potential Rejector. You will need to learn the Art of Apology. And you will need the skill to efficiently utilize the Reject-Me Formula.

Selecting a Promising Potential Rejector

Everybody in the world is a Potential Rejector—even small children and domestic animals.

The trouble with children and animals, unfortunately, is their well-known lack of discrimination: they will reject anybody at all, for no reason at all, and any rejection so easily won can hardly be highly valued. (In emergency situations, where no more promising Potential Rejector can be found, of course, a child or an animal may have to be used. In such cases it should prove helpful to remember that young babies can generally be counted upon to cry when you pick them up, and that cats can always be counted upon to walk away from you if you evidence a sincere desire to pet them.)

---

* See *The Telephone as an Instrument of Torture,* Chapter 6.

Adult human beings make the best Potential Rejectors, though, particularly those who can belittle you in areas of greatest personal vulnerability—e.g. sex appeal, professional competence, social poise, intelligence, tact, sense of humor, or any area in which you possess the least self-confidence. Needless to say, your most promising Potential Rejectors are those who are some sort of authorities in their particular fields of rejection—e.g., headwaiters or attractive young women.

The Apology as an Aid to Rejection

Once you have found yourself a Promising Potential Rejector, you must be able to let him know that you are someone who wishes to be rejected.

The best way to accomplish this task is to subtly put yourself down—to say something in an apologetic, self-deprecating manner which couldn't possibly be mistaken for false modesty. After all, hardly anyone is going to be foolish enough to like you if you've made it obvious that you don't even like your*self*.

There is an Apologetic Style suitable for every level of development, from the beginner's

"You'll have to forgive my appearance this evening"

to the more advanced student's

"You probably think I always look this bad."

There is also an Apologetic Remark suitable for every occasion. For example, to a dinner guest you might say:

(1) "This martini probably isn't dry enough for you, but we do have all this vermouth and we're almost out of gin."

(2) "Tonight is the first time I've ever tried this dish, so it probably won't be any good."

(3) "I'm afraid I made the coffee too strong."

(4) "I'm afraid I made the coffee too weak."

(5) "I hope you don't mind—the meat is a little too well done."*

(6) "It may not taste so bad to you, but this isn't the way it's *supposed* to taste."

When telling a joke you might say:

(1) "I'm afraid this story is a bit long-winded."

(2) "I guess this anecdote doesn't have much point."

(3) "The guy who told me this tells it a lot better than I do."

---

* It hardly pays to apologize for meat that's too rare, since it could always be put back on the stove.

FIG. XIV: SAMPLE SELF-DEGRADING GREETING CARDS

When out for the evening with someone you could say:

(1) "I wanted to take you to a better place but I couldn't get reservations."
(2) "You're probably used to taller men."
(3) "I meant to wash my hair but I didn't have time."
(4) "I couldn't seem to find a pair of pantyhose that didn't have a run in them."
(5) "I'm probably boring you with all my problems."
(6) "I'm sorry I'm not more articulate."
(7) "I'm usually a lot more fun to be with."
(8) "My hands don't usually perspire so much."

The rule in all the above suggestions is: *Always call attention to something embarrassing which wouldn't otherwise be noticed.*

To the apprentice apologizer we must give the following warning. It frequently happens that, just as you're preparing to deliver an apology, somebody beats you to the punch by *complimenting* you about the very thing you were going to apologize for.

How to handle this frustrating situation? The solution is a simple one: *Confide a Secret Personal Embarrassment which invalidates the compliment.*

SECRET PERSONAL EMBARRASSMENT #1:

"You really have a terrific figure."

"Thanks, but my legs are much too fat."

SECRET PERSONAL EMBARRASSMENT #2:

>"You really have terrific legs."
>
>"Thanks, but my ankles are much too thick."

SECRET PERSONAL EMBARRASSMENT #3:

>"That's a sensational outfit you're wearing."
>
>"I'm surprised you like it. I bought it eight years ago at a rummage sale and I can hardly stand to look at it anymore, but I had to wear it because everything else I own is absolutely filthy."*

We would advise the serious student to do his advanced research in Japan, where he can readily learn to formulate such self-deprecating remarks as:

>"Please forgive the humble appearance of my unworthy home and the unwholesome quality of my disgusting and overripe food."

The Reject-Me Formula and How to Use It

All forms of the basic Reject-Me Formula are really tests —repeated requests for votes of confidence. Naturally, any time you ask somebody for a vote of confidence you run the risk that he will actually give it to you.

---

*Alternate reply: "It's not even mine."

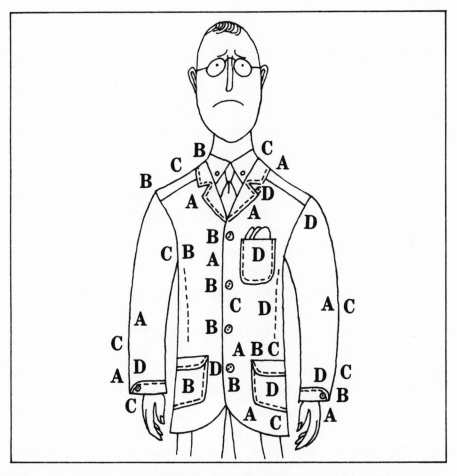

FIG. XV: THINGS TO CONTEMPLATE IMMEDIATELY AFTER PURCHASE OF APPAREL

(A) Locations of probable premature fraying; (B) points of weakest construction; (C) places most likely to be soiled; (D) styling details most likely to be disapproved of by friends or business associates.

With the following formula, the chances of experiencing such a mishap are remote, to say the least.

REJECT-ME MOVE #1: *Ask for a vote of confidence in a way that suggests you don't deserve to get it.*

REJECT-ME MOVE #2: *Refuse to accept any vote of confidence, ask again, and be sure to make rejection the easiest response.*

REJECT-ME MOVE #3: *When you succeed in winning a rejection, however slight, act terribly hurt—thus assuring future rejections.*

An illustration of this formula follows.

REJECT-ME MOVE #1:

YOU: "I suppose you already have plans for tonight?"

REJECTOR: "Nothing definite—why?"

MOVE #2

YOU: "Oh, well, we were thinking of having some people over, though I don't really know how interesting you would find them. You do have these other plans, then, do you?"

REJECTOR: "Well, yes, we did sort of promise these people. Maybe some other time, though."

MOVE #3:

YOU: "You never seem to have time for us anymore, now that you're successful."

The above conversational maneuver was a successful example of the Invitation type of rejection. That is, rejection was accomplished by forcing someone to decline your invitation. A slight variation of this maneuver—using the same Reject-Me Formula—is the Evaluation type of rejection. In this case, rejection is accomplished by forcing someone to give you an unflattering evaluation of yourself.

REJECT-ME MOVE #1:

YOU: "Tell me frankly, what do you think of me? Be perfectly frank."

REJECTOR: "I think you're very nice."

MOVE #2:

YOU: "No, tell me exactly what you think. I admire frankness more than any other quality."

REJECTOR: "Well . . . to be perfectly honest I do think you act a little neurotic at times."

MOVE #3:

YOU: "Is that so! And I suppose you think *you're* perfect?"

Needless to say, not all rejections are quite as easily won as the two examples cited above. Most people, unfortunately, are rather reluctant to reject you. For one thing, most people are fairly kind, and rejecting you would make them feel uncomfortable and sad. In addition, rejecting you would add to their own already heavy burdens of guilt, thus making it necessary for them to adopt even more intensive programs of personal self-torture than before.

So then: How to handle the reluctant rejector?

How to Handle the Reluctant Rejector

The best way to deal with someone who seems determined to give you a vote of confidence by accepting an invitation of some kind from you is to offer him that invitation in such an embarrassing, self-deprecating manner that he couldn't possibly accept it without descending to the same humiliating level.

We illustrate by developing our first example.

YOU:	"I suppose you already have plans for tonight?"
REJECTOR:	"Not at all—why?"
YOU:	"Oh, well, we were thinking of having some people over. I guess it's kind of short notice, though."
REJECTOR:	"Not really. We didn't have any particular plans—"

YOU: "I'm so embarrassed. It's not even for dinner. We invited these two couples for dinner, you see, and there really wouldn't be enough food for everybody."

REJECTOR: "Oh, well, that's perfectly all right. We planned on eating home tonight anyway."

YOU: "I'm afraid I'm actually paying off a lot of social obligations tonight—"

REJECTOR: "Oh?"

YOU: "Yes, my husband keeps complaining we only have people over that *I* like, so tonight I thought we'd have some people over that *he* likes."

REJECTOR: "I see."

YOU: "Listen, don't feel you have to be polite and say yes if you have anything you'd rather do."

REJECTOR: "Mmhmm. Well, now that you mention it, I do remember some sort of promise to visit my in-laws later this evening. You know how those things are."

YOU: "No, listen—don't apologize. To tell you the truth, I didn't really expect you to be very anxious about coming over to see us anyway."

Test Problem: The Stalemate

A man and a woman return from a date. The idea of going up to her apartment for a nightcap has occurred to both of them. They are now outside her building. Each is moderately skilled in Reject-Me Technique. Here are the moves so far:

SHE: "I don't suppose you'd care to come upstairs for a nightcap?"

HE: "Well, I don't know. It's awfully nice of you to ask, I mean, and I'd really like to, but I'm sure it's too late. Isn't it?"

SHE: "I guess so. It's . . . let's see . . . one o'clock. That's probably too late for you, isn't it?"

HE: "Well, it's not too late for *me*, but I'll bet *you* generally like to get to sleep around this time. Right?"

SHE: "Well, I don't usually get to sleep till after two. But I'll bet *you're* exhausted. Aren't you?"

HE: "Well, *I'm* not tired, but what's the sense in forcing *you* if *you* are?"

SHE: "Well, *I* could stay up a little bit longer, but *you* really look like you're dying to get home and get some sleep. Aren't you?"

HE: "Well, *I* could, but I doubt that *you* could."

SHE: "Well, *I* could, but I doubt that *you* could."

HE: "Well, *I* could, but I doubt that *you* could."
        Etc.

PROBLEM: How to break the stalemate without losing the rejection?

SOLUTION: Either party may reply, in a somewhat hurt voice:

"Well, it's obvious you don't really want to, so let's just forget it till you're more in the mood."

Chapter 5: How to Lose Your Job

Now that you have mastered the rudiments of rejection you are finally ready to put classroom theory to practical use.

In this and succeeding chapters we shall show you how to use the Dynamics of Rejection to lose your job, your love-mate and your friends. In short, we shall enable you to systematically expel everybody you know from your life, leaving you wholly free to wallow in self-pity and climb ever higher on the ladder of Total Personal Misery.

The easiest area in which to begin is the area of employment.

Losing your job is not the simple matter you might imagine it to be. Chances are you were hired because you possess a certain skill. So, if only because it would take an unnecessary amount of time for your employer to find and train another person to replace you, he is not going to be so eager to let you go.

How, then, to instill in him this eagerness?

If you are able to look upon the act of being fired as the feat of making your employer reject you, then you can apply many of the rejection-inducing techniques you've already learned. You are already, so to speak, halfway to the unemployment office.

In this section we shall supplement what you already know with several On-the-Job Anxieties which should lead you right into basic Reject-Me Behavior for Employees.

Basic Underpaid Attitude

One attitude which translates readily into On-the-Job Anxieties and thence to Reject-Me or Fire-Me Behavior is the assumption that you are being underpaid.

If you brood long enough about being underpaid—making up a list of grievances and reciting them over and over again to yourself—you will work yourself up into quite a rage.

If you get furious enough, you may even wish to quit your job. *Do not quit your job.* If you quit your job you will miss out on all the satisfaction and righteous indignation of being fired.*

---

* The only time quitting might have to be considered is in an emergency—when all attempts to get yourself fired have failed.

What is the next step after you've decided you're being underpaid?

The next step is either to demand an absurdly high raise* or to attempt to balance the scales in some other manner.

Balancing the Scales

The best way to balance the scales is to work less. Come in late in the morning. Take unusually long lunches. Leave the office early in the day. Fill up the remaining time with coffee breaks and long-distance phone calls.

After a while you may begin to feel a bit uneasy about being caught. *Don't let this deter you.* Plenty of other people in your office are getting away with just as much. *They* aren't getting caught, and you can bet they aren't being underpaid either.

Continue to come in at 9:30 instead of 9:00, to come back from lunch at 1:30 instead of 1:00, to leave work at 4:30 instead of 5:00.

But perhaps after a week or two of such behavior, nobody has said anything to you about your new hours. *Why haven't they?* Can it be that you were being underpaid even worse

---

* For proper Bluff Form, see *Relationship-Destroying Maneuver #2: The Great Marriage Bluff,* Chapter 7.

than you thought—that your employer's conscience is so guilty he can't even bring himself to reprimand you? Well, then, you're just going to have to try a little harder, aren't you? *You're just going to have to find out exactly how much you'll be allowed to get away with, because that's the only way you'll be able to tell when the scales have been balanced.*

Begin coming in at 10:00. Return from lunch at 2:00, or even 3:00, if necessary. Leave the office at 4:00. (Perhaps soon you won't even have to take off your coat between the time you arrive in the morning and the time you leave for lunch or between the time you come back from lunch and the time you go home for the day.)

And now you have created a curious sort of situation. You still believe you are being underpaid—apparently worse than anybody in the office, since nobody has yet had the guts to give you any meaningful reprimands. However, for the amount of work you are doing, you are being vastly *overpaid*. You know you have stepped way out of line. And yet you are unable to stop. How could you possibly, of your own accord, give up that extra time in bed in the morning or the chance to do all those errands in the afternoon—especially when others are getting away with it too? Obviously, you can not.

This is the time for you, in a state of frenzy, to start trying to cover your tracks. Sneak in and out of the office when no one is looking. Prepare elaborate excuses for your hours away from the office—appointments with the opthalmologist, with the osteopath, with the peridontist, with the podiatrist, with the endocrinologist.

Cover your entrances and exits with imaginative subterfuges: Keep your coat in the washroom downstairs to make it seem as though you have just stepped out for a moment. Arrange for somebody you can trust to switch on your desk lamp promptly at 9:00 A.M. and mess up your desk a little then to straighten it up and turn off your light at 5:00 P.M.

Dread and yet somehow long for that inevitable summons to your employer's office which will end forever this absurd nightmare of deception.

Finally, one day it will happen. The ultimate rejection. The ultimate relief. You will be fired. You'll be given two weeks' severance pay and asked to leave immediately. And as you clear out your desk, you will know all the suffering satisfaction of the martyr—the profound pleasure of knowing you have been horribly, unjustly punished and rejected.

Quiz

Question: The unemployment office has arranged for you to be interviewed by a prospective employer, and has asked that you show him samples of your work. What should you say when you present this work?

Answer: "This isn't really my best work, but I never had time to re-do it." Or: "This really could have been good if they hadn't made me change it."

Chapter 6: How to Avoid Deep Romantic Relationships

In Chapters 6 and 7 you will learn how to get rejected by Lovemates or Potential Lovemates on all levels of involvement. In this chapter, at the most basic level, you will first learn how to repel members of the opposite sex at parties. Next, assuming you have been unsuccessful at that level of rejection and have actually been asked for your telephone number or obtained somebody else's, we will show you how to get the most misery out of dating.

And finally, should you be unable to avoid a Deep Relationship or marriage, Chapter 7 will furnish you with enough strategy to eventually get rid of even the most ardent lover, wife or husband.

Misery at Parties

Parties organized primarily for the purpose of meeting eligible men or women are, by their very nature, ideal opportunities for self-torture and misery.

The very act of walking into a house full of people you don't know, who are talking and drinking and laughing merrily among themselves and who didn't even notice you come in, immediately places you in a position of almost esthetically perfect vulnerability.

For you are then truly lost. And, as you go through the elaborate stalling-for-time rituals of hanging up your coat, fixing yourself a drink and lighting up a cigarette—while searching desperately for a familiar face and finding none— you realize that you are going to have to walk right up to a total stranger and introduce yourself, and you must then ask yourself the inevitable question: *Why on earth would anybody want to talk to me?*

This question is entirely valid. Why *would* anybody want to talk to you—unless you believe that you are both brighter and more beautiful than whomever they are talking to at present. And if you believe that, this book will never be able to do a thing for you.

Very well. Once you have posed the above question to yourself, you have two alternatives:

(1) You could go and stand in the corner by yourself and wait for somebody to walk over and strike up a conversation.

(2) You could go over to the host, whom you probably know at least by name, and try to get *him* to talk to you.

Let's assume you do the latter. The host will be hustling

drinks and hors d'oeuvres, catching up on past events with people he hasn't seen in a long time and, in general, talking to guests who are more interesting than you. He will give you a perfunctory hello, pull you over to a small group of people who are entirely engrossed in one another, quickly introduce you and then disappear. The people he has introduced you to will smile blandly, possibly ask you one polite question, and then return to their previous conversation without waiting for your reply.

You are now free to go and stand in the corner by yourself and wait for somebody to walk over and strike up a conversation.

If nobody does, you can lean against the wall and nurse your drink until the ice cubes all melt. You can pretend to be fascinated with the pictures on your host's wall or with the titles of the books or records on his shelf, or you can go into the bathroom and study the contents of his medicine cabinet or, better yet, you can study the asymmetry of your face in his bathroom mirror.

However, let's imagine that somebody is actually inconsiderate enough to ignore your Acceptance-Prevention strategy by just walking up to you and striking up a conversation. How do you handle him?

Here is one effective device, modeled loosely on the Reject-Me Formula outlined in Chapter 4.

The No Small-Talk Maneuver

This maneuver, like all Reject-Me Formulas, is essentially a three-move Evaluation Rejection. This is how it works.

REJECT-ME MOVE #1:

YOU: "I hate parties. I never know what to say to anyone. I guess I just can't make any small talk."

GUEST: "Really? I think you're doing very nicely."

MOVE #2:

YOU: "No, I'm afraid I'm not very interesting to talk to. I suppose you'd rather be talking to someone else."

GUEST: "Oh, not at all. I'm enjoying this conversation immensely, I really am."

YOU: "Well, you're very kind, but I'm sure I'm boring you to death."

GUEST: "Not at all, not at all. (PAUSE) But I *am* getting rather thirsty. Why don't you just sit right over there while I go and freshen my drink?"

MOVE #3:

YOU: "If you're that anxious to get away from me, I'm certainly not going to try and stop you."

But let's say that, despite the use of the above techniques, you have met somebody, somebody nice—somebody too nice to be interested in you, no doubt. But the two of you seemed to have a lot in common, you seemed to enjoy talking to one another, and you were unable to make yourself sufficiently repulsive to preclude the possibility of further contact.

A telephone number has been asked for and given out, and now a phone call seems imminent. How to handle what comes next?

The Telephone as an Instrument of Self-Torture

Whether you're going to call for a date, or whether you're going to wait to be called, why not take a moment to ponder what a marvelous aid to anxiety the telephone actually is.

If you're waiting for an important call, you can neither leave the house nor call anybody else in the meantime, or else you'll miss it. Even if you have an answering service, you'll probably miss it—answering services are very whimsical about which of your calls they pick up, which messages they remember to give you, and in what form they give them to you. And answering machines often fail to record certain messages, or else the caller doesn't speak loudly or clearly enough and you don't know what he's saying, or he starts speaking before the beep and you miss most of his message, or the tape runs out and you miss the whole thing.

The telephone, when you do speak on it, effectively strips your personality of all its non-audio charm—all smiles and winks and other facial expressions that help to convey subtlety and clarify your meaning. And God help you if you don't have a beautiful voice.

Then, too, when you speak on the telephone you never know quite what's going on at the other end of the line. You can't see the facial expressions of whomever you're talking to, so you really never know where you are with them. Perhaps they're bored. Or dripping wet. Or watching television. Perhaps they've put the receiver down and walked away. Perhaps someone else is with them, listening to what you're saying, and they're both exchanging funny faces and other signals, and they can scarcely contain their laughter about what you're saying.

Perhaps you're saying something unflattering about a third party and just at that moment he was making a call, his line got crossed with yours and he overheard everything you said about him.

Perhaps your wire is being tapped and what you're saying is being recorded and transcribed, and you'll see it all on paper some day in court.

With all this in mind, let us now proceed to the actual grisly business of telephone invitations for dates.

Waiting for a Phone Call

Let's say you are the young lady in this case. (We know that as a result of the women's movement, men can now experience all the misery of waiting for phone calls, just as women can now experience all the misery of making them, but please let us express it this way because it's simpler, O.K.?) How can you make yourself completely miserable while you wait for the young man's call, and perhaps even discourage him from asking you out once he *does* call?*

Begin by assuming that if the young man *is* going to call you, it will be on the day after the party, some time after work. *But* (and this is your first anxiety) *does he know how late you work?*

He does not. Suppose he calls you shortly after 5:00 P.M. and then again at about 5:30, and he doesn't find you in either time because you work till 5:30 and don't get home till 6:00. *Will he try again at 6:00?*

Maybe he won't. After all, an attractive man like that

---

* At this point you may wish to turn back to Chapter 1, review the section on *The Power of Negative Thinking* and use it as a pattern for rumination and Anxiety Formation.

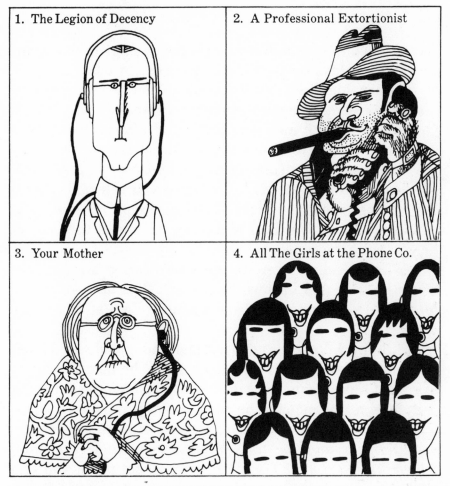

1. The Legion of Decency

2. A Professional Extortionist

3. Your Mother

4. All The Girls at the Phone Co.

FIG. XVI: PEOPLE WHO MIGHT BE SECRETLY LISTENING IN ON YOUR TELE-
PHONE CONVERSATIONS

doesn't need to spend all his time calling up girls who aren't ever home. Maybe you should leave work at 5:00, just to be on the safe side. But what if you should get tied up in traffic? Maybe you should sneak out at 4:30. Better yet, why not say you're feeling sick and take the whole afternoon off? That way you'll be *sure* to be home when he calls.

That is the next step, then: *You must take off the entire afternoon and wait for his call.* Station yourself right next to the telephone and don't leave it for a second, not even to go to the bathroom. Needless to say, by the end of the evening he will not have called.

What a fool you were to think he'd call at all. As if you were the only girl in town he'd ever asked for a telephone number. How many numbers did he collect at that party *alone?*

Still, he did ask for your number and he did say "I'll call you," and nobody forced him to do that. The fact that he did ask must have meant he was at least *considering* calling you —at least at the moment he asked for your number.

Maybe you said something between the time he asked for your number and the time he said goodnight—something which disgusted him. Try to remember what it was you said. Probably all you said was "It was nice meeting you." Surely there's nothing wrong with telling a person it was nice *meeting* him.

And yet, you never know. Giving him your number *and* telling him it was nice meeting him might have been a little pushy.

Maybe he just asked you for your number so he could get away from you gracefully. Not a bad little anxiety. But here's a better one:

Maybe he has been trying to call you all night and the phone just hasn't rung because it's out of order. You must find out if this if true. Pick up the phone—and don't be disappointed when you hear the dial tone. Just because you hear a dial tone doesn't mean your phone is working. You must conduct a more conclusive test.

Call a girlfriend. When she answers say, "Don't ask me to explain, just call me right back," then hang up. Don't be dismayed when she calls you right back. At least you now know the phone is working.

This is the moment for your next anxiety: *Maybe he was trying to call you while you were checking to see if the phone was working and he got a busy signal.*

Enough anxieties for a single night. Go to bed.

The next day, decide he's never going to call and don't leave work till the regular time. But just as you arrive home and are about to open your door, you might hear the phone ringing. Scramble frantically for your keys. Your purse will fall to the ground and the contents will spill all over, but somehow you'll manage to get the key into the door while the phone is still ringing, and you'll just have time to race across the room, trip on the throw rug and pick up the receiver before the ringing stops.

This is the moment to decide that you don't care if he ever calls—that you're not going to spend the rest of your life glued to a lousy telephone just because some creep at a party said he might call you.

Just go about your normal evening routine. If he calls, fine, and if not, that will be fine, too. Make yourself some dinner. Eat it in front of the TV. Wash the dishes. Dry the dishes. Wash your hair. Dry your hair. And do everything you would normally do if you were just staying home and not expecting anyone to call. But turn off the water in the sink and in the tub and switch off the dryer every four minutes because you thought you heard the phone ring.

Maybe the reason he hasn't called you is that he simply hasn't been home. Maybe you should look up his number in the phone book and just give him a call, and if he isn't home you'll know that's probably why he wasn't calling you, and if he *is* home you can just hang up.

This is not a good idea. Here is a better one:

Maybe you gave him the wrong phone number. After all, how often do you call your own number? You might have gotten it wrong—reversed the last two digits or something.

106

And if he did call and found out you'd given him the wrong number he probably thought you did it on purpose. The poor man! How hurt he must feel! What can you do? You can call him, that's what you can do.

Look up his number in the phone book. You find it, but now you have another problem—there are three people listed with the same name. What a fool you'll sound like, trying to find out if you've called the right one: "Excuse me, but are you the person who took my incorrect telephone number at a party the other night?"

This is clearly not the way to go about it. What you must do is dial each man in turn, strike up a conversation based on something you discussed at the party, and then if it's the wrong man you can just hang up, and it won't be that embarrassing because he won't know who you are. *Unless, of course all three of them are cousins and the one you talked to calls the other two and tells them.*

This is an absurd anxiety. Go ahead and call, just as you planned.

But while you're getting up the nerve to call, the phone rings. It's him! Start to reach for the receiver, then check your hand in mid-air. Why pick it up on the first ring? Do you want him to know how anxious you are? Let it ring twice. Better yet, let it ring three times. Now pick it up. And there's nobody there.

How do you feel—letting him get away when he finally got home and called you! Well, now you surely have to call him. Quickly, before he leaves the house again!

Try the first number. And you're in luck—it's the right man!

Tell him who it is. Say: "Did you just now try to call me?" There will be an embarrassed silence. "I'm afraid not," he'll say.

Phoning for a Date

Now let's say you are the young man in this situation.

An attractive young lady has given you her phone number and you said you'd call her, and now it's time for a few anxieties.

First of all, how do you know she wants to go out with you? Sure, she gave you her number, but what else could she have done when you asked her? She's probably praying you won't use her number.

No, that's an absurd idea—she's not praying you won't use her number. Because she doesn't even remember *giving* you her number, and she certainly won't know who you are when you call. Not only that, but when you call you're going to catch her at an awkward moment. Like . . . *like when her boy friend is there.*

That's it—she already has a boy friend. How could such an attractive girl not already have a boy friend? Well then, there's no point in calling her, is there, just to ask her out and have to be told she already has a boy friend?

No, that's ridiculous. If she *did* have a boy friend she would have had a perfect excuse not to give you her phone number. She could have just said: "I'm sorry, but I already have a boy friend."

So it looks like you're going to have to call her after all.

What will you say to her? You'll probably run out of things to say to her in the first thirty seconds. You'll say "How are you?" and she'll say "Fine, how are *you?*" and you'll say "Pretty good, thanks," and then that'll be it. You won't be able to think of a single other thing to say. There'll be a terrible silence, you'll blurt out some awkwardly phrased invitation to go out, she'll refuse you in some humiliating manner, and then she'll tell all her friends how dumb and awkward and gauche you are.

Maybe you could avoid all that by jotting down a few opening remarks and then just read them to her in a fairly natural-sounding voice.

Opening Remarks for Telephone Calls

There are two types of opening remarks for any telephone call in which you plan to be rejected: Primary Opening Remarks and Secondary Opening Remarks.

Here are two acceptable forms for Primary Opening Remarks:

(1) "You probably don't remember me, but—"

(2) "You'll never guess who this is."

Both remarks are excellent setups for rejections. They both suggest you're so unmemorable that the person you're calling *won't* ever guess who you are.

A good Secondary or Follow-Up Remark is one *which gives the person you're calling the best possible chance to avoid talking to you.* Thus:

(1) "I guess I'm calling at a bad time, huh?"

(2) "You sound like you were just walking out the door."

(3) "I'll bet I caught you right in the middle of dinner, didn't I?"

(4) "I'll bet I woke you."

(5) "Do you have a moment to talk now? Should I call back some other time when it's more convenient? Or would you prefer that I didn't bother you at all?"

The Invitation

There are two effective types of rejection-inducing invitations.

(1) The invitation that hasn't been extended far enough in advance for the person you're inviting to accept, even if she wants to go:

> "Can you go to a New Year's Eve party—tonight?"

(2) The invitation that has been extended so far in advance that the person you're inviting cannot gracefully decline if she *doesn't* want to go:

> "Can you go to a movie with me three weeks from Thursday?"

We prefer the latter invitation, since it has the added advantage of displaying a lack of confidence so degrading that it taints anyone who might accept it.

Which brings us to form.

The proper form for a rejection-inducing invitation, as pointed out in Chapter 4, is one where the person invited cannot accept without placing herself in a humiliating position. Here are two variations of this form:

(1) *"What are you doing* Saturday night?"

(2) *"Do you have any plans for* Saturday night?"

The only way to accept such an invitation is to reply:

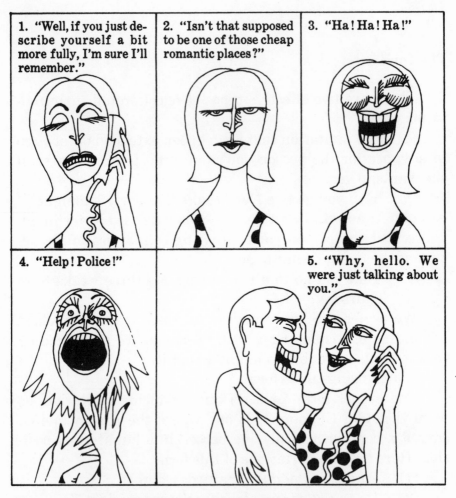

FIG. XVII: POSSIBLE FEMALE RESPONSES TO REQUEST FOR DATE

Anticipate one or more of the above reactions before speaking to feminine Potential Rejectors.

"I don't have a thing to do Saturday night unless you ask me out."

The person replying also faces the danger that the above question wasn't an invitation at all, but merely a casual inquiry into her popularity.

Once it has been established that the person you are inviting is willing to accept your invitation, the final step is to make whatever you have planned sound as unappealing as possible. Thus:

(1) "Some guys I know are throwing a party, and they're kind of creeps, but it might not be that bad. Do you want to go?"

(2) "My uncle gave me these two free tickets to this concert, which will probably be pretty boring, and the seats aren't too good either. I don't suppose you have any interest in going, do you?"

The Ordeal of Actually Going Out

If, despite the stratagems offered above, you've gotten yourself a date, then you have to face the ordeal of going out.

There's still some hope for you, however. You may still be able to ruin the evening, have a miserable time, and make certain that your date will never go out with you again.

How to accomplish this task?

Ten Ways to Kill a Good Evening

(1) If you're a girl, don't be ready when your date arrives. Make him wait at least a half hour—especially if he is anxious to get to a play or movie at a specific time. If you live alone, make him wait in the hall. Otherwise, see to it that he is entertained by your roommate, your parents, or any shaggy, friendly pet which will leave hairs of a contrasting color on his suit.

(2) If you're a man, show up late and without any plans for the evening. Ask: (a) "What do you feel like doing tonight?" (b) "Do you feel like going to a movie, or what?" (c) "Which movie do you feel like going to?" Etc.

(3) If you're a girl, kill any plan for the evening that your date suggests. Thus:

KILL #1:

"Let's go somewhere and dance."

"I'm not a very good dancer."

KILL #2:

"Let's see a play."

"I never understand what they're about."

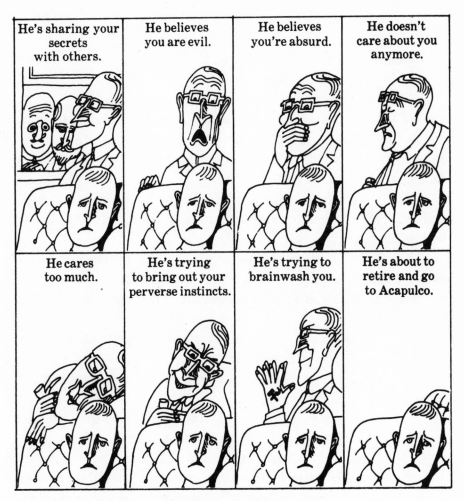

FIG. XVIII: APPROVED FEARS ABOUT PSYCHOTHERAPISTS

To prevent psychotherapy from undoing all the good this training manual is doing for you, visualize the above situations during your sessions.

"Let's go out for Chinese food."

"Chinese food always makes me break out."*

(4) If you're a man, speak about your aversion to marriage. If you're a girl, tell him how desperate you are to get married and what type of religious education you expect your children to have.

(5) Talk about your own faults or those of your date. Criticize him or her for smoking or drinking, or for *not* smoking or drinking.

(6) Talk about psychoanalysis. Tell him about your own if you're in it, and urge him to get into it too. If he's already in analysis and you aren't, make fun of him and urge him to get out of it.

(7) Make fun of any romantic gesture your date makes at any time during the evening.

(8) Quiz him or her about anybody of the opposite sex who walks by and says hello.

(9) Talk about anybody else you've gone out with, are going out with, or would like to go out with.

(10) In a restaurant, ask your date for a bite of whatever he or she is eating. After you receive it, ask for another. Then another. Then another. Sooner or later, even the ten-

---

* This is a good opportunity to combine a Kill with a Secret Personal Embarrassment.

derest of hearts will petrify at your requests, and rejection will be inevitable.

Misery in Sex

There are four basic areas in which you can make yourself miserable about sex: (1) availability of partners, (2) your equipment, (3) your performance, and (4) disease.

Availability of Partners

Let's face it, there just doesn't seem to be anybody suitable out there anymore. Everybody you know is either terminally boring or extremely unattractive or married or gay. Try as you might, you just can't seem to meet anybody new, and when you do, no sooner do you start telling them all about yourself, about all your problems and the marvelous way you're learning to cope, than their attention begins to wander and they begin looking around the room and yawning.

Maybe you should move to another city or something.

Your Equipment

Get hold of a copy of *Playboy* if you're a woman, *Playgirl* if you're a man, and compare your body and your primary and secondary sex organs to those of the ordinary people pictured in these magazines. Better yet, get hold of some XXX-rated videotapes. Is your equipment as big, firm, long, thick, and nicely shaped as theirs? If not, how can you bear to even have anybody see you naked?

Your Performance

To get the most misery out of sex, it should be staged as a theatrical event or an athletic contest. You've heard about Type A behavior in cardiac cases. Try to be a Type A lover— that is, competitive, anxious, and obsessed with your performance. Not only must you see to it that you and your partner both have orgasms every time you make love, you must have them neither too soon nor too long after commencement of foreplay, and, needless to say, you must have them simultaneously.

Your performance should always be compared to performances in the past—your own and those of your mate's previous lovers. If you like, you and your partner could rate each other's performance by means of a little bedside chart or by the cards used to grade Olympic gymnasts.

Disease

In the old days, the only diseases you had to fear from sex were syphilis and gonorrhea, either of which could be cured by a shot of penicillin. Not much to worry about there, unfortunately.

Things were going too well, especially with the advent of the sexual revolution. People were getting relaxed about sex for perhaps the first time in history, having it more often and with more people, and definitely having more fun. *Too* much fun, some folks thought.

So along came herpes to spoil the fun. Herpes can take years to surface, and there's no cure for it. You can agonize about catching herpes from a new sex partner, or, if you have herpes already, you can agonize about how and when to tell prospective lovers, or whether to tell them at all, and make yourself pretty miserable in the process.

But, let's face it, the most you can ever hope to get from herpes is a few gross pimples and a little itching. Not too much to worry about there either.

No, herpes was not the answer. People still sought something to take the joy out of sex, to punish themselves and others for the fun they were having.

Finally, along came AIDS to fill the need.

At first, AIDS didn't seem like much either. Oh sure, AIDS is always fatal. Oh sure, there's no cure. But the only groups initially at risk from AIDS were promiscuous male homosexuals, Haitians, heroin addicts, and hemophiliacs. This is not to say that if you were a promiscuous male homosexual, a Haitian, a heroin addict, or a hemophiliac that you didn't have plenty to worry about, only that AIDS was not initially a real mainstream kind of worry.

Well, now it is. Now anybody in the world—heterosexual men and women included—can be a carrier of AIDS, and you may never know until about five years after you slept with them if they were. You may never know unless you develop some of the following symptoms: cold, flu, fever, chills, rapid weight loss, swollen glands, diarrhea, constant fatigue.

So it hardly matters anymore that there are no suitable available partners out there, it no longer matters how you rate your equipment, it no longer matters how you rate your performance. These days, to sleep with anyone new is, quite simply, to flirt with death. (There are reportedly a number of people who already have AIDS, who are so angry and bitter that somebody gave it to them that they continue to have sex with unsuspecting partners, figuring, "If *I* go, *everybody* goes.")

Celibacy seems to be about the only answer for you. And when you're celibate, just think of all the time you're going to have to sit around and make up lists of everyone you've ever been to bed with who might possibly have had some contact with somebody who had AIDS.

Quiz

1. Problem: You are a young man calling a girl you don't know for a blind date. How can you phrase your opening remark so as to guarantee a rejection?

Answer: "Hello, you don't know me, but a guy you used to go to school with gave me your number, although I must say he thought you'd be married by now. How come you're not?"

2. Problem: You are a girl who has accepted a blind date, and the young man has just asked you how he will know you when he sees you. How should you phrase your reply?

Answer: "I'm a little on the heavy side. Also, I have a cold sore."

Chapter 7: How to Destroy Deep Romantic Relationships

To the layman it might seem that the deeper the relationship you have with someone, the harder it is to find misery and achieve rejection.*

We professionals are happy to report, however, that this is not the case—that, in fact, the reverse is true. The deeper the involvement, the more numerous are the opportunities for misery. Or, to put it more abstrusely: as involvement increases arithmetically, potential misery increases geometrically.

This by no means suggests that getting your lover, wife or husband to reject you is an easy matter. On the contrary, the chances are that it will be quite difficult for you to

---

* For advanced study in Destroying Deep Romantic Relationships, we recommend the recently published *How to Avoid Love and Marriage* by Dan Greenburg and Suzanne O'Malley.

achieve, unless approached in a sufficiently oblique and underhanded manner.

Why?

Well, to begin with (and regardless of whether or not you believe it), your lovemate is probably pretty fond of you. For another, he or she is no doubt just as eager for *you* to be the destroyer of your relationship.

To make absolutely sure it will be you and not your lovemate who is ultimately boosted up that ladder to Total Personal Misery, we have provided you with several deadly Relationship-Destroying Maneuvers.

Relationship-Destroying Maneuver #1: The Great Love Test

This maneuver can be used at any stage of a Deep Relationship, but it seems particularly well suited to the beginning stages of a romance, so we recommend it as your first major stratagem.

This maneuver, as well as the ones which follow, is, of course, based on the Reject-Me Formula.

REJECT-ME MOVE #1:
YOU: "Do you love me?"
MATE: "Yes, of *course* I love you."

MOVE #2:

YOU: "Do you *really* love me?"

MATE: "Yes, I really love you."

YOU: "You really *really* love me?"

MATE: "Yes, I really really love you."

YOU: "You're *sure* you love me—you're absolutely *sure?*"

MATE: "Yes, I'm absolutely sure."
(PAUSE)

YOU: "Do you know the meaning of the word love?"
(PAUSE)

MATE: "I don't know."

YOU: "Then how can you be so sure you love me?"
(PAUSE)

MATE: "I don't know. Perhaps I can't."

MOVE #3:

YOU: "You can't, eh? I see. Well, since you can't even be sure you love me, I can't really see much point in our remaining together. Can you?"
(PAUSE)

MATE: "I don't know. Perhaps not."
(PAUSE)

YOU: "You've been leading up to this for a pretty long time, haven't you?"

The reader will note that in this exchange the primary device is *a simple request for reassurance which, when given, is ignored.**

In this respect the technique is identical to the primary move of the Reject-Me Formula and, presumably, it could stand up alone as an effective Relationship-Destroying Maneuver. That is, you could just keep repeating the question "Do you love me?" until your lover, out of boredom, irritation or nausea, stops saying "Yes." However, it is the introduction of the philosophical question "Do you know the *meaning* of the word love?" that really *sets up* the rejection.

It is important to point out here that you need not strive to complete the whole maneuver on your first try. You may elect to stop just *before* Move #3, having gotten your love-mate to admit that he or she perhaps doesn't love you. This, after all, is quite a little victory in itself and could keep you brooding and sulking for several days. Then, when you have decided that you're ready for more self-punishment, you could begin the maneuver all over, either stopping again before Move #3 or pushing right on to victory.

---

* For best results, this maneuver (and all other tests for affection) should be used when the party to be tested is wholly absorbed in some activity like passing a long line of traffic on the highway with a truck approaching in the passing lane at seventy miles per hour.

Relationship-Destroying Maneuver #2:
The Great Marriage Bluff

This maneuver, like the previous one, may be used at any point in the relationship, but it is most effective in the earlier stages.

The Bluff Formula, while still a variation of the Reject-Me Formula, is essentially a two-step maneuver and breaks down as follows:

Move #1 is a demand for something either inappropriate or unreasonable. Move #2 *ignores warnings the bluff can't succeed and tops the demand with a harsh ultimatum.*

Thus, the question

"When are we getting married?"

if answered in some vague manner, may be followed by

"Either we set the date right now
or we stop seeing each other."

If you have been sufficiently clever in your timing, your love-mate's reply should come out as planned:

"Then I guess we stop seeing each other."

The Great Marriage Bluff, while a particular favorite with women, has been known to work for men just as nicely.

Relationship-Destroying Maneuver #3: Do We Have Anything Left?*

As you will notice from the opening line of dialogue below, you are to use this maneuver directly after an argument, preferably your first. You may even wish to combine it with one of the other maneuvers in this section—perhaps as a direct follow-up of *The Great Love Test.*

REJECT-ME MOVE #1:

YOU: "Well, our first big fight."

MATE: "Yes."

(PAUSE)

YOU: "Do you think we have anything left?"

MATE: "What do you mean?"

YOU: "I mean do you think we still have a relationship?"

MATE: "Of course. (PAUSE) Why—don't *you* think so?"

MOVE #2:

YOU: "Well, I thought so *before,* at any rate."

MATE: "What's *that* supposed to mean?"

YOU: "That I thought so *before.*"

---

* Maneuvers #3, #4 and #5 are equally effective for married couples. But then, so is Maneuver #1.

MATE: "What's *that* supposed to mean?"

YOU: "That I thought so *before*."

MATE: "And you don't think so *now*?"
(PAUSE)

YOU: "I don't know. What do *you* think?"
(PAUSE)

MATE: "I don't know. I thought so before."

YOU: "But now you're maybe not so sure, is that it?"
(PAUSE)

MATE: "I don't know. Maybe not."

MOVE #3:

YOU: "Well, since you're obviously planning to break up with me sooner or later, you might as well do it sooner and not prolong the agony."

Here again, as in *The Great Love Test,* Move #3 may be saved and used the next time you decide to run through the maneuver.

Please note that Move #3 plants the notion that your lovemate has been "obviously planning to break up" with you sooner or later. Though patently ridiculous, this idea will very likely be accepted by both of you, at least subconsciously, from that point on.

FIG. XIX: THINGS TO CONTEMPLATE AFTER EXTENDING OR ACCEPTING A PRO-POSAL OF MARRIAGE

(1) The possibility that right after you're married you'll meet the perfect mate. **(2)** The likelihood that prolonged domesticity will induce monumental boredom. **(3)** The pain and expense of divorce. **(4)** The things a family will keep you from doing. **(5)** The possibility that each of you will grow at different rates.

Relationship-Destroying Maneuver #4:
Don't Leave Me

This is a variation of Relationship-Destroying Maneuver #1. Instead of repeating the question "Do you love me?" it repeats the entreaty "Don't leave me" until your love is groggy from vain attempts to reassure you.

If you follow the tenth "Don't leave me" with the demand for tangible *proof* of your lover's intent to remain with you, this in itself might end the relationship. At the very least, it will plant the notion of leaving you where it probably did not exist before.

A slight variation of this maneuver is the observation "Some day you'll leave me." Innocuous enough at first, this observation with constant repetition becomes a self-fulfilling prophecy, and just as effective as "Don't leave me."*

---

* The *Don't Leave Me Maneuver* was first utilized in another form by Brer Rabbit to trick *his* adversary into throwing him into the Briar Patch.

Relationship-Destroying Maneuver #5: Attractive Fred (Counterpart for Women: Attractive Corinne)

There are two ways of dealing with the suspicion that your lover, wife or husband finds a friend of yours more attractive than you.

The first method is to repeatedly express this suspicion to him or her. Sincere jealousy is, we admit, a rather rudimentary means of achieving rejection, but it is nonetheless an effective one.

The second method is not only to *conceal* your jealousy but to bend over backwards to *prove* you're not jealous. What you sacrifice in immediate humiliation here you more than make up for in Long-Term Pain.

Such a method is the *Attractive Fred Maneuver*. It, like *Don't Leave Me*, requires a fairly long incubation period, but it is the most grueling of the maneuvers in this chapter, and therefore the most rewarding.

To get you in shape for the *Attractive Fred Maneuver* we suggest a little exercise called *Tell Me About Your Past*. This exercise begins by saying to your lovemate,

"Tell me about your past—
don't hold anything back"

and goes merrily on from there. After working out with *Tell Me About Your Past* for several weeks you will become so jaded that you will no longer find any misery in detailed descriptions of your partner's past loves. It is then time to try *Attractive Fred.*

Just how far you wish to carry this maneuver will depend upon your degree of sophistication, your threshold of pain, and how sincere you really are about seeking Total Personal Misery.

YOU: "Fred certainly seems to be attracted to you."

MATE: "Oh, really?"

YOU: "Yes. He's a pretty attractive guy himself, don't you think? Physically, I mean."

MATE: "Oh, I don't know. I suppose so. I haven't given it too much thought, to tell you the truth."

YOU: "I'll bet you've wondered what it would be like to go out with him."

MATE: "I can't really say I have."

YOU: "Come on. You can't make me believe the thought has never crossed your mind."

MATE: "No, it really never has. Not till now, at any rate."

YOU: "Not till now, eh? (PAUSE) I'll bet you *would* like to go out with him though. Wouldn't you?"

MATE: "Not particularly."

YOU: "You mean to tell me you wouldn't be even a little curious to find out what it was like—even if you could do so without hurting me?" (PAUSE)

MATE: "I . . . don't know."

YOU: "Well, I just want you to know that if you ever should decide you *are* curious, I think you ought to go right ahead and do it."

MATE: "You do?"

YOU: "Just to find out what it's like. Just to get it out of your system."

MATE: "You really wouldn't mind?"

YOU: "Mind? Of *course* I'd mind. But I'd much rather you just go ahead and do it and find out what it's like than *not* do it and have it become a fixation. You see what I mean?"
(PAUSE)

MATE: "Yes . . . I see what you mean."

Test Problem

Imagine that before you even have a chance to set your lovemate up for a Relationship-Destroying Maneuver, he or she begins to set *you* up for one. What sort of counter-strategy can you devise to halt each of the five maneuvers before you are forced into rejecting your lovemate?

Compare your solutions to the Counter-Maneuvers suggested below.

Counter-Maneuver to THE GREAT LOVE TEST:

> MATE: "Do you love me?"
>
> YOU: "It never would have occurred to you to ask that question unless you weren't sure you loved me yourself."

Counter-Maneuver to THE GREAT MARRIAGE BLUFF:

> MATE: "When are we getting married?"
>
> YOU: "Just as soon as you can convince me you will never look at—or talk to—another man."

Counter-Maneuver to DO WE HAVE ANYTHING LEFT?:

> MATE: "Do you think we have anything left?"
>
> YOU: "Is this your roundabout way of telling me you're through with me?"

Counter-Maneuver to DON'T LEAVE ME:

> MATE: "Some day you'll leave me."
>
> YOU: "There's no one who'd have me if I did."

Counter-Maneuver to ATTRACTIVE FRED:

> MATE: "Fred certainly seems to be attracted to you."
>
> YOU: "How can you be so blind—it's *you* he's attracted to."

Chapter 8: How to Lose Any Remaining Friends

We can safely assume that by this time you have gotten rid of your job and your lovemate.

Now it's time to go to work on your friends.

The Acceptable Failure Range

It is true that you can always go to your friends to share your joys or sorrows, and they will provide a perfect audience. It is also true that if you have *too many* joys or sorrows you are in great danger of losing that audience.

Let us put this more graphically.

It is apparent from the chart that if your goal is to *keep* your friends you must stay within the Acceptable Failure Range, but if your goal is to *lose* your friends you must exceed the Acceptable Failure Range in either direction.

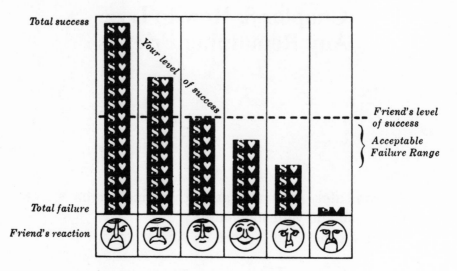

FIG. XX: FRIEND'S REACTIONS TO YOUR SUCCESS

Since you have already lost your job and your lovemate you will be exceeding the range in a downward direction.

Remind your friends what a failure you are. Call them up every day, several times a day. Complain. Despair. If possible, cry.

Reprimand them for not calling you up enough, for not

FIG. XXI: ESSENTIAL BROODING EQUIPMENT FOR ADVANCED PRACTITIONERS

(A) Lifetime tally of cigarettes smoked; **(B)** arc light or sodium vapor light for exaggerating facial blemishes; **(C)** mirrors for observing progress of bald spot; **(D)** optional photograph of self before nose job; **(E)** precariously poised expensive crystal drinking glass; **(F)** unrepaired electrical appliance; **(G)** box of old love letters from someone who rejected you; **(H)** dental and chest x-rays in light-box for intensive scrutiny; **(I)** telephone (see section *The Telephone as an Instrument of Self-Torture*); **(J)** shoes too tight to wear, too old to return, and too new to throw out; **(K)** photos of successful classmates, with estimated annual income; **(L)** obituaries of people younger than you; **(M)** insurance company life expectancy chart with used-up days crossed off.

caring. Accuse them of deserting you in your time of need. Act terribly, terribly hurt.

If you keep this up with any diligence, before you know it you will be . . .

Alone at Last!

Congratulations! You have driven everybody you know out of your life. Unencumbered by job, lover or friends, you are now free to brood twenty-four hours a day about how rotten life is and how everybody betrayed you in the end, just as you always knew they would.

With the aid of the techniques outlined in this book—*The Creation of Anxieties* and *Making People Reject You*—you have now achieved the ultimate: Total Personal Misery. And you have been punished for all your guilt.

Or have you?

About the Authors

Dan Greenburg is the author of several best-selling books, including *How to Be a Jewish Mother* (the #1 best seller of 1964 and still in print), *How to Make Yourself Miserable, Scoring, Love Kills, What Do Women Want?, How to Avoid Love and Marriage,* and, most recently, *Confessions of a Pregnant Father.*

His books have been translated into a dozen languages. His articles, stories and reviews have appeared in such periodicals as *The New Yorker, Esquire, Playboy, Ms, Life, New York Magazine, The New York Times Book Review,* and *The New York Times Magazine* and have been reprinted in 26 anthologies of humor and satire in the U.S. and England. (Three of his articles have won the Playboy Humor Award, and one of them was the most popular article in Playboy's first 25 years of publication.)

He is a co-author of the musical revues *Free to Be . . . You and Me* and *Oh! Calcutta!* (which is, at 17 years, the second longest-running musical on Broadway). His one-act plays have been produced Off-Broadway and at the Actors Studio, Yale University, the American Conservatory Theater, and elsewhere.

Feature film adaptations of four Greenburg books are currently in the works, including a French production of *How to Be a Jewish Mother,* which was a recent two-year hit as a play on the Paris stage.

Mr. Greenburg has written screenplays for the movies *Private Lessons, I Could Never Have Sex with Any Man Who Has So Little Regard for My Husband,* and (co-written with Suzanne O'Malley) *Private School.*

Mr. Greenburg is frequently seen on network television, on shows such as *The Today Show, The Tonight Show, Late Night with David Letterman,* and *Donahue,* as both author and stand-up comedian, and had a serious dramatic role in Frank Perry's film *Doc.*

He was born and raised in Chicago, got his B.F.A. from the University of Illinois, and his M.F.A. at U.C.L.A. He is married, is a recent father, and has been living in New York City since 1962.

Marcia Jacobs has been living quietly for the past eighteen years on the San Andreas Fault. In between tremors, she has written three humor books, contributed to various national magazines and newspapers, and numerous network and cable TV shows.

Ms. Jacobs lives with two cats she's afraid will leave her for a younger owner.